YORK NOTES

General Editors: Professor A.N. Je..
of Stirling) & Professor Suheil Bushrui (*American
University of Beirut*)

Francis Scott Fitzgerald

THE GREAT GATSBY

Notes by Tang Soo Ping

MA (MALAYA) *Lecturer in English,
University of Malaya*

LONGMAN
YORK PRESS

We are grateful to the following for permission to reproduce copyright material:

the author's agent, Laurence Pollinger Ltd, The Bodley Head Ltd and the Estate of the late
F. Scott Fitzgerald for extracts from the *The Great Gatsby* by F. Scott Fitzgerald.

YORK PRESS
Immeuble Esseily, Place Riad Solh, Beirut.

LONGMAN GROUP UK LIMITED
Longman House, Burnt Mill, Harlow,
Essex CM20 2JE, England
and Associated companies throughout the world.

First published 1980
Sixth impression 1987

ISBN 0-582-78124-8

Produced by Longman Group (FE) Ltd
Printed in Hong Kong

Contents

Part 1

Introduction

Literary background: the novel

The novel as a literary form emerged at the beginning of the eighteenth century in England, during the age of the Industrial Revolution. The rise of the middle class created a demand for simple reading material, based on familiar everyday experiences. The novel, therefore, developed as a piece of prose fiction that presented characters in real-life events and situations. Daniel Defoe's *Robinson Crusoe* (1719), Samuel Richardson's *Pamela* (1741) and Henry Fielding's *Tom Jones* (1749) are some examples of early novel-writing.

The novel of manners

The portrayal of actual life and conditions brought about an interest in manners (social behaviour and attitudes) as they were associated with certain classes of people of a certain time and place. And from this kind of interest there came into being the novel of manners such as those written by Henry Fielding and Jane Austen. This type of novel is based on the satirical and comic portrayal of a particular social class and the events concern the conflicts between individual attitudes and conventional values. In a way, most novels reflect the social manners of a certain class, of a specific time and place setting. But if these novels cover more than just social attitudes, then they cannot and should not be classified as novels of manners.

The romance

Whereas the novel is a piece of prose fiction that faithfully attempts to present life as it really is, the romance is a piece of prose fiction that describes life as it is imaginatively seen. Thus, whereas the novel adheres closely to real life as it is daily experienced, the romance plunges into the unfamiliar and inner aspects of human nature, which are not often encountered in normal life. The romance, therefore, is not concerned with ordinary events. It penetrates into the inner depths of man and establishes a moral truth about human nature.

The Great Gatsby: novel of manners or romance

On one level *The Great Gatsby* may be read as a novel of manners. If we see Gatsby's idealism as representing a personal code of conduct which opposes society and its values, the book can be called a novel of manners. The tone, too, is satirical and comic most of the time.

But bearing in mind the wider significance of *The Great Gatsby*, it is more appropriate to classify it as a romance. For the book does not merely show the different values of two groups of characters. The account is more concerned with the portrayal of a man's idealism seen, on the one hand, in all its magnificence and, on the other, in all its unreality. The imaginative presentation of Gatsby as a mysterious figure fits well with the fantasy and magic of his dream. And the very elusiveness of his dream points to the true condition of man's lot, the fact that hopes and desires can never be fully realised.

The author

Born in 1896 in St Paul, Minnesota, Francis Scott Fitzgerald was a Mid-Westerner (see p.10) and he came from a family which, on his mother's side at least, had its roots in the Middle West. Phillip McQuillan, his maternal grandfather, was a successful businessman in St Paul. Although Fitzgerald's own father, Edward Fitzgerald, came from Maryland, he subsequently settled in St Paul and started a business there too in 1898. The Fitzgeralds left St Paul in 1903 but they returned in 1908. And St Paul continued to play its part in Scott Fitzgerald's own life and career. It was here that he came to complete his first novel, *This Side of Paradise* (1920). After his marriage to Zelda Sayre, he settled for some time in St Paul and it was here that his daughter was born. In his novels, especially *The Great Gatsby*, St Paul, or the Mid-West at least, was to contribute a considerable influence on the shaping of the characters' moral outlook.

Edward Fitzgerald belonged to the urban middle class. After a promising start in business, he became more and more of a failure as he moved from job to job. Whatever money Edward Fitzgerald and his family had came from Phillip McQuillan, the father-in-law. Scott Fitzgerald's own education from St Paul Academy to Princeton University was mostly paid for by his mother's family.

The young Fitzgerald was never more conscious of his poverty than in 1915 when he met Ginevra King, a girl who belonged to a wealthy Chicago family. The father, a successful broker, disapproved of Fitzgerald's poor background, and Ginevra subsequently married another man, the most eligible bachelor in Chicago at the time. The unhappy experience left Fitzgerald with a painful awareness of his poverty and a sense of social inferiority. It contributed to the persistent yearning and awe with which he regarded the rich. But the event also warned him of the ruthlessness and carelessness of the upper class.

Fitzgerald was subsequently called to the army in 1917 and was not discharged until 1919. It was during this time that he met and became engaged to Zelda Sayre. Fitzgerald's prospects, however, were still not very bright. Zelda therefore broke the engagement and Fitzgerald, rejected a second time, returned to St Paul. Here he completed his first novel, *This Side of Paradise*. The book was published in 1920 and became a best-seller. He returned to Zelda and this time married her. Evidently, Gatsby's loss of Daisy and his return to her life is derived from Fitzgerald's own experience with Zelda and with Ginevra King as well.

Life with Zelda was a whirl of gaiety and lavish spending. The Fitzgeralds recklessly pursued their pleasures from America to Europe and back, wildly living up to the post-war mood of careless enjoyment. And it was during this period that Fitzgerald wrote *The Beautiful and Damned* (1922), another novel, *Tales of the Jazz Age* (1922) which is a collection of short stories, *The Great Gatsby* (1925) and others.

The gaiety and high living, however, did not last long. Zelda suffered from schizophrenia, a form of mental disorder that is characterised by a breakdown in rational thinking. (There is also a separation between the mind and the emotions, so that the patient's feelings and emotions do not correspond to the actual situations of his or her life.) After the first break-down in 1930, she became progressively ill and had to be confined in a mental hospital. Fitzgerald was further troubled by financial and psychological problems caused by his wife's extravagance and jealousy of his writing. The fact that his later novel, *Tender is the Night* (1934), completed around this time, was not the triumph he had expected it to be must have worried him even more and deepened his fear of disaster. This sense of defeat and failure was complete, especially after his inability to succeed even as a film scriptwriter in Hollywood. *The Crack-up*, a series of essays written in 1936, is a moving analysis of his failure. He tried to make a come-back into the literary scene with a novel, *The Last Tycoon* (1941), but he died of a heart-attack in 1940 while trying to complete it. Fitzgerald died without recapturing the triumph and the success of his youth.

Many critics have seen Fitzgerald's artistic achievement in terms of his ability to depict American society, its history and its people. *The Great Gatsby*, especially, is often taken as an account of the story of America. It describes how the American idealistic outlook, that is, its belief in life and spiritual happiness, contrasts with an interest in material advancement and possessions (see p.11). Fitzgerald's concern, however, was more personal. In *The Great Gatsby*, as in his other novels, he was writing of his own experiences. If his story recalls a historical situation, this merely broadens and increases the significance of his writing.

Fitzgerald's life was full of contradiction. To begin with, he was an idealist; he idealised youth in the sense that he regarded youth as the most precious and most beautiful period of life. It is a time of hope, when everything seems possible and life seems to be full of opportunities. Fitzgerald's own youthful success encouraged this belief. Even before he was thirty years old, he had written three successful novels. And yet even in his earliest writings there is a fear, a sense that young dreams may come to nothing. So in *This Side of Paradise* and in *The Beautiful and Damned* youthful hopes are checked by the realisation that reality could never measure up to ideals and dreams.

Fitzgerald thought that there should be no waste of youth's talents and opportunities. He emphasised the need for self-discipline to make the most of resources and advantages. And yet this was the same man who repeatedly wasted his literary talent by becoming a magazine writer. In his twenty-year career, he wrote about a hundred and sixty short stories for magazines. Fitzgerald himself was conscious of his own misuse of talent. He wrote in *The Crack-up*: 'I have been only a mediocre caretaker of most things left in my hands, even of my talent.'*

His contradictory nature is also to be seen in his attitude towards money. His rational self, influenced also by his experience with Ginevra King, made him disapprove of and condemn the rich whom he regarded as ruthless and cruel. But his gayer side admired and envied them and this gave rise to a secret sense of his own inferiority. His life of extravagance and gaiety may therefore be seen as an imitation of the way of life of many rich people.

To the very last, these two contradictory sides of his character remained with him and they continued to shape his life and novels. But what Fitzgerald has done in *The Great Gatsby* is to see his own nature in its two aspects and to work out a situation in which they are identified with two opposing groups of people—one thriving on dreams, the other living by physical pleasures.

Fitzgerald's life, therefore, influenced his writings in several ways. The attitudes he conveys are essentially mixed, reflecting his own emotional and rational responses all at the same time. In *The Great Gatsby*, for example, his dreamy idealistic self can be identified with Gatsby's imagination and hope, even as his rational mind criticises it through Nick Carraway. The situations that occur in his writings were usually drawn from his personal life, for example, Gatsby's desire for

*F Scott Fitzgerald, *The Crack-up*, ed. Edmund Wilson, New Directions, New York, 1956, p.71.

Daisy, his participation in the war at Montenegro, his expensive way of living and so on. In addition, Gatsby's and Nick's Mid-Western origins parallel Fitzgerald's own; for instance, Nick's father, who leaves only advice but no money, is not unlike Edward Fitzgerald.

As for characters, these were also drawn from the writer's personal background. But what is significant is that Fitzgerald's characters were not singly or directly related to people in real life. For part of Fitzgerald's success as a novelist lies in the way in which he was able to combine several familiar people into one character, so that what emerged was a 'composite character'.* Gatsby, for example, is a combination of the writer himself, a friend called Max Fleischman and 'some forgotten farm type of Minnesota'.† Gatsby, therefore, is sensitive and imaginative even though he is also naive, flashy and sinister.

Elsewhere, however, the writer divides himself into several characters. While his idealistic self was contained in Gatsby, his objective, critical mind was identified with Nick. Then too, his attitude towards wealth was divided between Gatsby's yearning to be part of Daisy's world and Nick's total abhorrence to the Buchanans. These are only some of the ways in which Fitzgerald used personal events and experiences. They show how his technique combines the subjective or emotional and the objective or rational. The kind of double view so achieved which looks 'from within and without'‡ is what gives his writing its depth and balanced judgement.

Background notes

The Jazz Age

The 1920s in America, the period just after the First World War, is known as the Jazz Age, the Roaring Twenties, the Aspirin Age and so on. The period is usually identified with money and gaiety. This was the time of jazz music, the Charleston (a dance) and the motor car (called the automobile in the United States). Gatsby's flashy cars, his lavish parties, the reckless conduct of his guests and the carelessness of the Buchanans are all part of this atmosphere of gaiety and wild enjoyment. Coming just after the war, the high living and merrymaking are usually seen as a reaction to recent suffering. Fitzgerald wrote on this social

*John Kuehl, 'Scott Fitzgerald's Critical Opinions', *Modern Fiction Studies*, I, no. 1, Spring 1961, p.17.
†Ibid, p.17.
‡F. Scott Fitzgerald, *The Great Gatsby*, with commentary and notes by J.F. Wyatt, The Bodley Head, London, 1967, p.33. All subsequent references will be to this edition, unless otherwise indicated.

scene in *Tales of the Jazz Age* and in *Flappers and Philosophers* (1921). Related to this atmosphere of wild celebration was the rise of organised crime. Illegal gambling and bootlegging (that is the production and sale of illegal liquor), were rife in the United States at the time and led to wide-spread corruption. Even sports became occasions for bribery and cheating. In 1919 the World Series, which was a series of baseball games, was manipulated with the bribing of the Chicago team. This background of crime and illegal dealing prevails in *The Great Gatsby*. Jay Gatsby is suspected of being a bootlegger and a murderer, Meyer Wolfshiem is said to have 'fixed the World's Series' (p.64) and Jordan Baker is characterised as a woman notorious for cheating at golf.

The 1920s also brought new life to literature. The war and experience in Europe had given the young Americans a new maturity and a broader outlook. And because these writers (including Fitzgerald himself, Ernest Hemingway (1899–1961), William Faulkner (1897–1962) and others) had been freed from their narrow home atmosphere and were informed by their European experiences, the literature which they produced was more spirited and significant. It expressed the truth as it was felt by the writers who, uninhibited by American values and attitudes, could see American habits and outlooks objectively and so write about them frankly.

The Mid-West

The term is actually 'The Middle-West' and refers to states lying west of the Appalachian Mountains and north of the Mississippi River Basin. The Mid-West states include North Dakota, Gatsby's home-state, and Minnesota where St Paul, Fitzgerald's home town, is sited.

For Fitzgerald, the Mid-West is identified with the hopeful spirit which Gatsby represents. (Fitzgerald's own idealism is related to his Mid-Western background). For it is in the Mid-West that Fitzgerald sees still a certain old-fashioned stability which rests on the comfort of old, unchanging values and close relationships, where some of the old pioneer spirit of industry and purpose still lingers. Gatsby's Mid-Western origins, therefore, are significant. And Nick's sympathy for Gatsby is partly explained by the fact of his similar Mid-Western background. The Buchanans, however, although originally Mid-Westerners, have lost that 'gift for hope' (p.6). Having lived longer in New York, they have become more like the people in the East (the East referring to the Eastern Seaboard). They have surrendered totally to a careless, aimless way of life, occupied only with material things. And it is this difference between the East and the Mid-West, a difference, that is between materialistic concerns and spiritual purpose, that destroys Gatsby.

The American Dream

The American Dream describes an attitude of hope and faith that looks forward to the fulfilment of human wishes and desires. What these wishes are, were expressed in Thomas Jefferson's Declaration of Independence of 1776, where it was stated:

> We hold these truths to be self-evident, that all men are created equal, that they are endowed by their creator with certain unalienable rights, that among these are life, liberty and the pursuit of happiness.*

This search for freedom and happiness actually goes back to the very beginning of American civilisation, to the time of the first settlers. The Puritan Fathers who first came to New England (one of the first states to be settled), the Quakers who came to Pennsylvania (another American state), and the Huguenots in Virginia were all religious refugees who were driven to the New World by persecution. To these people, America represented a new life of freedom, holding a promise of spiritual and material happiness. For those settlers who were not so religiously inclined, America was still a fairyland, a land of great possibilities. It was also a rich mine of natural resources. And so the first thirteen colonies came into being, amidst the religious and materialistic hopes of the first settlers. Material prosperity and progress kept pace with religious and spiritual goals because the Puritans and the Quakers alike approved of industry and material advancement. For, whereas physical pleasures were evil, hard work and achievements were regarded as indications of inner goodness.

When the Eastern Seaboard, comprising the thirteen colonies, became overcrowded, this pursuit of happiness and freedom shifted inland with the drive westward beyond the Appalachian Mountains. The opening of the Middle and Western states increased the sense of hope and faith. And this looking forward beyond the immediate present, this belief in the future, has become a national characteristic that may partly explain the speed of American advancement in so many areas of activities. The democratic system, first voiced in Jefferson's Declaration of Independence in 1776, may be traced to this basic attitude of hope and confidence.

The American Dream, however, originally relates to a desire for spiritual and material improvement. What happened was that, from one point of view, the material aspect of the dream was too easily and too quickly achieved, with the result that it soon outpaced and even obliterated the early spiritual ideals. So there emerged a state of

*Walter Allen, *The Urgent West: The American Dream and Modern Man*, E.P. Dutton, New York, 1969, p.4.

material well-being but lacking in spiritual life or purpose. So that when Fitzgerald produced Gatsby, modelled no doubt on the writer's own faith in life, he seemed to have created a character who represented an early American in whom the Dream was still very much alive.

From another point of view, the American Dream has totally failed to bring any kind of fulfilment, whether spiritual or material. For all the progress and prosperity, for all the declaration of democratic principles, there are still poverty, discrimination and exploitation. And as for values and morality, there are also hypocrisy, corruption and suppression. In a way *The Great Gatsby* is also a comment on this condition. Other writers have written about these hard truths which have made the American Dream an illusion; John Steinbeck (1902-) in *The Grapes of Wrath* (1939) and J.D. Salinger (1919-) in *The Catcher in the Rye* (1951) are two examples.

A note on the text

Textural history

In July 1922 Scott Fitzgerald expressed his intention 'to write something new—something extraordinary and beautiful and simple and intricately patterned'*. Out of this desire *The Great Gatsby* was created. It took ten months to complete and during this time Fitzgerald made every effort to keep away from drink. He stopped all other writing that he considered trashy in order to devote himself to the new work.

The manuscript was sent to Scribner's, the publishers, at the end of October 1924 but Fitzgerald still had to revise his book considerably before it was finally ready for print. He added Chapter II to the original work, rewrote Chapters VI and VII and made some significant changes and additions in Chapter VIII. He had wanted to call the novel *Trimalchio* but finally settled for *The Great Gatsby*.

The first edition was published in 1925.

Modern editions

Some modern editions of *The Great Gatsby* include the following:

The Great Gatsby, with commentary and notes by J.F. Wyatt, The Bodley Head, London, 1967. Page references in these notes are to this edition.
The Great Gatsby, Scribner, New York, 1968.
The Great Gatsby, Penguin Modern Classics, Harmondsworth, 1969; 1971.

*Andrew Turnbull, *Scott Fitzgerald*, The Bodley Head, London, 1962, p.138.

Part 2

Summaries
of THE GREAT GATSBY

A general summary

Nick Carraway, a man from the Mid-West, comes to New York to work as a bondsman. Here he meets Daisy, his second cousin, and her husband Tom Buchanan. He hears about his next-door neighbour, a mysterious man called Jay Gatsby, who gives fabulous parties at his house.

Nick soon learns that Tom Buchanan has a mistress, Myrtle, whose husband is the car mechanic, George Wilson. He becomes acquainted with Jordan Baker, a friend of the Buchanans. He also gets invited to Gatsby's parties and meets his host in person. Jordan tells Nick that five years ago in Louisville, Daisy's home-town, Gatsby had met and fallen in love with Daisy. But he was a soldier then, and was called to serve overseas. Daisy subsequently married Tom. Now five years later, Gatsby has found Daisy again. He has purposely bought his house which is across the bay from Daisy's, so that he can be near her. Through Jordan, Gatsby asks Nick to invite Daisy to tea so that he can meet her again. He has hoped that Daisy would come to one of his parties (given solely for this purpose) but so far she has not appeared. Nick agrees and Gatsby gets to meet Daisy at last.

In the meantime Nick learns more about Gatsby's background and his business activities. He also discovers that Gatsby has risen from a penniless beginning to achieve wealth and power with the help of a rich man called Dan Cody. But, mostly, Gatsby owes his success to his own faith in life and his optimistic confidence in himself. Nick finds then that Gatsby's intense desire for Daisy is part of his absolute belief in life and the happiness it holds in store for him.

As his relationship with Daisy grows, Gatsby meets Tom. But Tom is contemptuous of Gatsby, whom he regards as his social inferior. When Tom discovers that Gatsby is secretly involved with his wife, he immediately forces a confrontation between them. Daisy, after some persuasion from Tom, admits that she has loved her husband in the early days of their marriage. However, she tells Gatsby that she has loved him too and still loves him now. But this is not good enough for Gatsby. He still wants Daisy to say that she loves only him and that she will leave Tom to marry him. Tom, however, exposes some of Gatsby's criminal activities and Daisy is frightened. She refuses to listen to

Gatsby's denials and decides to leave the Plaza Hotel where the whole group has been having drinks.

Daisy drives off first with Gatsby. When Nick, Tom and Jordan arrive at Wilson's garage they discover that Myrtle has been knocked down and killed by Gatsby's car. Nick later learns from Gatsby that Daisy had been driving the car, but Gatsby himself intends to take the blame. The next day Gatsby stays at home, waiting vainly for Daisy to call. By the time that Nick gets home from work, Gatsby has been killed, shot dead by George Wilson, Myrtle's husband.

Nick is left to prepare for Gatsby's funeral. He tries to get people to attend but no one appears except Gatsby's father and another man who was a former guest at Gatsby's house. There is no sign of Tom and Daisy. After the ceremony Nick decides to return to the Mid-West. He is tired of life in the East. But before he goes he meets Tom, and Daisy's husband admits having told George Wilson that Gatsby was the driver of the car in the accident.

As he leaves, Nick's last memory of Gatsby is of a man who has worked for an ideal and lost. And Nick realises that this is what man needs to do, to strive continuously for an ideal, even though the struggle may not bring his dream any closer.

Detailed summaries

Chapter I

Nick Carraway explains that it has always been a habit with him to be detached, to reserve judgement. But on the subject of Gatsby he is unable to withhold his admiration and awe. Although Gatsby represents everything he normally scorns, his absolute faith in life and his idealism win Nick's approval and sympathy. Nick abhors the things that happened to Gatsby.

Nick has left his Mid-Western home to come to work in New York. He is eager to experience life in the East and is ready to work hard to make his career here a success. He rents a house in West Egg, next to a palatial mansion. He is invited to dine with his second cousin, Daisy, and her husband, Tom Buchanan. They live in East Egg, where the rich have their homes.

Nick observes the wealthy surroundings in which Tom and Daisy live. He also notices that Tom is muscular, proud of his house and horses, and talks about the superiority of the white race. Daisy and her friend, Jordan Baker, laze around to pass the time. They chat with Nick and tell him a story about a butler's nose. Nick notices that Daisy's voice has a certain magical attractiveness about it.

Nick is mystified when Tom is called to the phone and Jordan Baker refuses to talk to him. She only wants to listen to Tom's conversation. He is told finally that Tom is speaking to his mistress.

Daisy later confesses to Nick that she is not happy. She is scornful of life and money. But Nick senses that Daisy feels a certain pride in saying all this.

As Nick leaves the Buchanans, he feels confused and disgusted. He cannot understand why Daisy does not leave Tom since he is keeping another woman. He is also disturbed by the feeling that Tom's actions are the result of some dissatisfaction with his life. It is as if he is searching for something to satisfy him.

On reaching home, Nick catches sight of his next-door neighbour standing outside his mansion of a house. As he watches, the figure reaches out his hands longingly towards a green light across the bay.

NOTES AND GLOSSARY:

Middle Western City: the reference to the Mid-West explains Nick's initial delight in coming to the East. The distinction between the East and the Mid-West is also matched by a difference in values and attitudes. This distinction is a significant one in the novel and one which Nick has yet to realise

New Haven: this is the town in Connecticut where Yale University is situated. The name is often used by Tom and Nick to refer to the university

Dodge: the name of an American car

movies: an American term referring to films, moving or motion pictures

Midas and Morgan and Maecenas: Midas was a legendary King who loved money and had the power of turning everything he touched into gold. Maecenas was a rich Roman. Morgan refers to J.P. Morgan (1827–1913), a very rich nineteenth-century American businessman and financier

like the egg in the Columbus story, they are both crushed flat at the contact end: on his third voyage to the New World, Christopher Columbus found a huge river flowing into the Gulf of Mexico. Since he believed that this river started from the 'top' of the earth, Columbus decided that the earth was not round as he had originally thought, but flat at the top

one of the most powerful ends that ever played football at New Haven: American football is different from English football. The 'end' refers to a forward player whose position is at the end of a line

There was an excitement in her voice that men who had cared for her found difficult to forget . . . a promise that she had done gay, exciting things just a while since and that there were gay, exciting things hovering in the next hour: this refers to the way in which Daisy attracts and holds men in her power by the magical quality of her voice. This may partly explain Gatsby's intense desire and adoration

'Gatsby?' demanded Daisy. 'What Gatsby?': this is the first time that Daisy hears Gatsby's name mentioned after five years, as Jordan tells Nick later in Chapter IV. Significantly, after this one question, Daisy does not refer to Gatsby again. This seems to indicate that Gatsby is no longer important to Daisy, and will later indicate the futility of his hopefulness about Daisy

'The Rise of the Coloured Empires': probably a reference to Lothrop Stoddard's *The Rising Tide of Colour* (1921)

'Do you want to hear about the butler's nose?': the story that Daisy and Jordan tell Nick is absurd and silly. It shows the way in which rich people like these pass their time in idle chatter

The Cunard or White Star Line: shipping companies specialising in the transatlantic routes

'From Louisville. Our white girlhood was passed together there': Louisville is a town in Kentucky. Daisy is making fun of Tom's ideas about the superiority of the white race

I was confused and a little disgusted: for a moment, Nick is shaken by what he has seen in Daisy's house. This, however, is not enough yet to spoil his sense of expectation about life in the East

he stretched out his arms towards the dark water in a curious way, and, far as I was from him, I could have sworn he was trembling: this is Gatsby's first appearance and it comes with an image of deep longing. This image will remain throughout, reminding the reader of his immense desire and faith.

Chapter II

Nick goes to New York with Tom one afternoon. On the way to the city, they pass by a desolate area of land which Nick calls 'a valley of ashes' (p.23). This dreary place is presided over by a huge signboard in the form of a pair of spectacles. As their train stops in this ghost valley, Tom insists that Nick gets off with him to meet his girl-friend.

Against his will, Nick is taken to a garage where he meets a pale, timid mechanic called George Wilson. While Wilson is trying to get Tom to sell his car to him, his wife Myrtle appears. Nick notices that there is a vitality, a liveliness, about her. She and Tom arrange to travel in the same train to New York. As they make their way to Myrtle's apartment, Nick notices that Tom's mistress dresses fashionably. She chooses a taxi that is lavender-coloured with grey upholstery. She calls her puppy a girl instead of a bitch.

Myrtle organises a party and Nick meets her sister Catherine and the McKees who live downstairs. Myrtle's behaviour becomes more and more affected. She talks about her disappointment with George whom she married thinking he was a 'gentleman', a man of breeding.

Nick learns from Catherine that Gatsby is probably related to some royal family. She informs Nick of her fear of the man. Nick also discovers that Tom has been misleading Myrtle into believing that Daisy is a Catholic who will not agree to a divorce.

Suddenly, Myrtle and Tom start to quarrel and fight. Tom will not allow his mistress to mention Daisy's name. Myrtle is slightly hurt and Nick, half-drunk by this time, leaves the apartment.

NOTES AND GLOSSARY:

the borough of Queens: a borough of New York City
Fourth of July: Independence Day in the United States of America
'Terrible place, isn't it?': Tom's words are ironical. The valley of ashes
                        is a physical representation of the kind of world in
                        which Tom himself lives, which is morally dead and
                        bare
car: the compartment or carriage of a train
drug-store: a store that sells soft drinks, cosmetics, magazines
                        as well as drugs (medicines)
taxicab: a taxi
John D. Rockefeller: John Davidson Rockefeller (1839-1937), a fam-
                        ous American oil tycoon
the Park: Central Park, New York
158th Street: streets in New York are mostly numbered
apartment: American word for a flat
**The living-room was crowded to the doors with a set of tapestried furni-
ture entirely too large for it, so that to move about was to stumble continu-
ally over scenes of ladies swinging in the gardens of Versailles:** the furni-
                        ture and decorations in Myrtle's house are showy
                        and overdone. They reflect Myrtle's desire to live
                        like the rich. However, together with the magazines
                        and papers lying around, they merely reflect
                        Myrtle's bad taste

Broadway: the name of a street in New York city on or near which most of New York's theatres are located

She pointed suddenly at me, and everyone looked at me accusingly. I tried to show by my expression that I expected no affection: this is one example of Fitzgerald's humour. The comedy underlines the seriousness of Myrtle's position

Beauty and the Beast: a significant reference to Daisy and Gatsby. In the fairy tale the Beast, like Gatsby, yearns for the love of a girl, but his ugliness always prevents him from winning her love. Although Gatsby is not ugly, his lack of social background and status also make him unattractive as a suitor. And in the end these are the things that count with Daisy

Chapter III

Nick describes the lavish celebrations that go on in Gatsby's house next door. The bustle of preparation, the abundance of food, the huge crowd that drifts in, the colour, the noise and the ravages left behind—these impressions of a fantastic, chaotic way of living come to Nick as he watches.

Nick himself is invited by Gatsby to one of these parties. He goes, expecting to meet his neighbour at last. But he finds himself lost in a carnival of people and noise. Feeling uneasy and confused, he meets Jordan and happily attaches himself to her. As they move around in the crowd, where hardly anybody knows anybody, Nick hears gossip about the host. He is rumoured to have killed a man once. He is even suspected to have been a German spy during the war.

Feeling uncomfortable with an arrogant group of people from East Egg, who evidently feel superior in West Egg, Jordan and Nick wander off in search of their host. But they come upon a man with owl-eyed spectacles in the library, and he voices to them his satisfaction that Gatsby's books are not fakes, used only for decorating the shelves. They are real books. And the man praises Gatsby for being so realistic.

As they rejoin the party outside, Nick and Jordan find themselves sitting with another couple. Nick mistakenly thinks the man is a fellow guest only to find that he is indeed Gatsby himself. Nick is struck immediately by the man's good-will, but he also sees a certain absurdity in his formal manner and speech. Gatsby is called away to the phone, and Nick finds himself asking questions about him. Jordan's vague answers recall the rumours that he has earlier heard. And when Nick sees Gatsby again, standing some distance away, he notices the man's aloofness from the gaiety that is around him.

Jordan is called away for a private conversation with Gatsby, and Nick, preparing to leave the party, observes the absurd behaviour of the guests. When Jordan returns she is still dazed from her talk with Gatsby. Hurrying off, she insists that Nick should telephone her the next day.

As Nick leaves the party, he comes across a car which has been driven into a ditch. Owl-eyes emerges from the car and is immediately mistaken for the driver. The driver himself, when he does appear, is untroubled by the near disaster. He is obviously drunk.

After this, Nick begins to review his activities in New York. He talks about his work, his fascination with the city and his growing relationship with Jordan. He dismisses Jordan's dishonesty at golf. Even when Jordan drives carelessly in a car that she has borrowed from a friend, Nick is quite undisturbed by her carelessness. He is attracted to her, but, out of a sense of honesty, is determined to break off from a girl back home before he gets more intimate with Jordan.

NOTES AND GLOSSARY:

hair bobbed in strange new ways: short hair styles were fashionable at the time

the Follies: a light theatrical show consisting of a medley of songs, dances and sketches, and produced by the famous Florenz Zicgfcld (1869–1932)

East Egg condescending to West Egg: a significant reminder of the social gap between the rich who reside at East Egg and those living in West Egg

'This fella's a regular Belasco': Belasco (1839–1931), a famous American actor, theatrical producer and playwright. He was responsible for bringing more realistic stage effects to American theatre. The owl-eyed man is so impressed by Gatsby's realism that he compares him with Belasco. The irony here is unmistakable

old sport: Gatsby's favourite phrase is English in origin. It is probably one he picked up during his Oxford days

the lower East Side of New York: the poor part of the city

a long duster: a full-length coat worn for driving

gas'line station: a petrol station

Chapter IV

Nick talks about the gossip created by Gatsby's mysterious background. He is said to be a bootlegger, he is still suspected to have killed a man, and he is supposed to be the nephew of a man called von Hindenburg.

The crowds, however, still flock to Gatsby's parties, uninvited. Nick lists down the kind of people who are Gatsby's guests—people who bear such names as Leeches, Bunsen, Civet, Stonewall, Dancies, Belchers and so on. Gatsby even has a guest who boards with him— Klipspringer.

One morning, Gatsby invites Nick to lunch with him in New York. This is the first time that Gatsby calls on his neighbour and Nick notices a certain restlessness about him. Soon Gatsby starts to talk about himself. He mentions his wealthy Mid-West family, his Oxford education, his travels and his war experience. Gatsby then informs Nick that he has a favour to ask. Jordan will talk to Nick on Gatsby's behalf.

As they near the city, Nick catches a first glimpse of it, full of beauty and promise. Then he sees a funeral procession.

During lunch, Nick meets Gatsby's friend Meyer Wolfshiem. Wolfshiem mistakes Nick for a business contact. He tells Nick that Gatsby is very careful about women. He is a kind of man who 'would never so much as look at a friend's wife' (p.63).

Nick soon learns that Wolfshiem is a gambler who had fixed the World's Series. He is utterly shocked at this betrayal of people's trust. Then as Nick and Gatsby leave the restaurant they meet Tom Buchanan. Nick introduces Gatsby to him.

That afternoon, Jordan tells Nick of Gatsby's love affair with Daisy five years ago. Daisy was the most popular girl in Louisville; her house had the biggest lawn. One day, Jordan saw her speaking to a military officer. Some time later Daisy was said to have been prevented by her family from going to New York to say goodbye to a soldier. She was quiet and unhappy from that winter to the next autumn. But she soon recovered and was engaged to Tom Buchanan before long. By June the following year, they were married. The night before her wedding, however, Daisy was found crying hysterically in her room. She had to be calmed and pacified. And the next day she married Tom as if nothing had happened.

The Buchanans were very happy at first and Daisy was very much in love. Then Tom met with an accident; there was a girl in the car with him. This, however, did not spoil his relationship with Daisy for long. They moved around from place to place, living a very gay life.

After this account, Jordan tells Nick that Gatsby has bought his house in West Egg to be close to Daisy. He wants Nick to invite Daisy to tea so that he can meet her again. After hearing this, Nick feels that, unlike Gatsby, he has no girl like Daisy to dream about. But he has Jordan.

NOTES AND GLOSSARY:

von Hindenburg: a German general who became the president of the German Republic

From East Egg, then, came the Chester Beckers: the guest list here is a humorous as well as an ironical presentation of a cross-section of the East Egg society—rich but ridiculous and superficial

The American Legion: a body of ex-servicemen. Wolfshiem later encourages Gatsby to join this organisation (p.148)

San Francisco: this is in the Far West, not in the Mid-West, so Gatsby is clearly lying here

trying to forget something very sad that had happened to me long ago: this does not refer to his affair with Daisy because his encounter with Daisy happens during the war, that is, later on

the night they shot Rosy Rosenthal there: Herman Rosenthal was a criminal who gave evidence about police corruption in New York. He was shot dead in June 1912, by a gang of men. A police lieutenant, Charlie Becker, was involved in the killing. He was subsequently charged and condemned

'Miss Baker's a great sportswoman, you know, and she'd never do anything that wasn't all right': this is extremely ironical because, as Nick has already established in the earlier chapter, Jordan is dishonest even in golf

'He would never so much as look at a friend's wife': another piece of irony. Gatsby, as it turns out, is very interested in another man's wife

Santa Barbara: then a fashionable holiday resort in California

'but she came out with an absolutely perfect reputation': note Jordan's mocking tone when she says this about Daisy and her way of life. The same cynicism is detected in her description of Daisy's shifting behaviour before and after her marriage to Tom. Jordan's attitude, therefore, contrasts with Gatsby's sentimental belief in love and in Daisy

Chapter V

Nick returns home that night after his talk with Jordan and finds Gatsby's house all alight. Gatsby has been looking over his house. Nick arranges with him the day on which he will invite Daisy to tea. Tactlessly, Gatsby tries to repay Nick for his help with a business offer which Nick rejects.

When Gatsby arrives on the appointed day, he is obviously nervous and absent-minded while waiting for Daisy to come. At one point, he almost gives up, saying it is too late, that Daisy will not be coming.

When Daisy does arrive, she thrills to the idea of a secret meeting with Nick, thinking that Nick is in love with her. Gatsby has disappeared from Nick's lounge; he knocks at the front door a few minutes later, as if he has just arrived. Nick leaves him to greet Daisy alone. But he tries to listen to whatever goes on. He only hears Daisy's voice speaking in artificial tones.

When Nick enters his lounge, he observes Gatsby's nervous behaviour. He keeps apologising to Nick for having upset an old clock on the shelf. Gatsby follows Nick into the kitchen and voices his agony and embarrassment. Nick reassures him and sends him back to Daisy. Leaving them alone, Nick wanders out of the house. When he returns, Gatsby is glowing with joy. He takes Nick and Daisy over to his house. He shows Daisy through the house, shows off his clothes, his swimming pool and his hydroplane. Daisy greets everything rapturously. As he watches Daisy moving about his possessions, Gatsby, at one point, is filled with a sense of wonder and disbelief at her presence. He almost gives way to hysterical laughter. Later, he points out to Daisy that from his house, he can see the green light that burns nightly at the end of her dock. Then Nick sees an old photograph of a man whom Gatsby explains is someone called Dan Cody.

Gatsby gets his guest, Klipspringer, to play on the piano and sing for them. As the latter sings a song about rich and poor people, Nick sees a look of doubt on Gatsby's face. He must have compared Daisy with the image he has created of her in his mind, and found her lacking. But Gatsby recovers from that moment of doubt; he and Daisy are soon absorbed in each other. They are not aware of Nick's departure.

NOTES AND GLOSSARY:

the whole corner of the peninsula was blazing with light: it is significant that Gatsby's house is at its brightest just when he is about to meet Daisy again. The brightness becomes an image of his happiness and excitement

the World's Fair: an international exhibition, where exhibits from various countries are displayed. Some well known examples are the London Exhibition of 1851, the New Orleans World's Fair of 1883 and the Chicago World's Fair of 1893

a green house arrived from Gatsby's: an example of Fitzgerald's use of comic exaggeration

Together we scrutinized the twelve lemon cakes from the delicatessen shop: the comedy in this scene relieves the tension but it also serves, by contrast, to underline the seriousness of this meeting between Gatsby and Daisy

'Is this absolutely where you live, my dearest one?': compare Daisy's careless gaiety with Gatsby's nervousness and anxiety

Castle Rackrent: the title of a novel by Maria Edgeworth (1767–1849) published in 1800. The plot traces events in an Irish household that is destroyed by riotous living on the part of several generations of the Rackrent family

The clock took this moment to tilt dangerously at the pressure of his head, whereupon he turned and caught it with trembling fingers and set it back in place: this event where Gatsby upsets a clock and puts it back in place represents Gatsby's attempt to re-arrange time so that the past is repeated in the present

like Kant at his church steeple: Emmanuel Kant (1724–1804), the German philosopher, was a man of regular habits, who refused to leave his native town, Konigsberg; he liked to remain among buildings and objects with which he was familiar

the Merton College Library: Gatsby or the original owner had modelled this room on this famous library at Oxford

'You always have a green light that burns all night at the end of your dock': we know now that the green light that Gatsby has been seen reaching out for, in Chapter I, is actually associated with Daisy

'One thing's sure and nothing's surer . . .': Klipspringer's song is significant here. Its comment on the difference between the rich and the poor is immediately followed by Gatsby's feeling of doubt. Nick thinks that his fear comes from the realisation that Daisy is not as he has imagined her to be. But Gatsby's fear may stem from the fact that Klipspringer's song reminds him of the gap between him and Daisy. Is he wondering whether his newly-acquired wealth is sufficient to help him bridge the gap?

Chapter VI

Rumours about Gatsby have been multiplying and his reputation has become quite notorious.

As Nick knows it, however, Jay Gatsby's life and career is remarkable. He was really James Gatz from North Dakota, whose parents were poor, unsuccessful farm people. From his youth on, James Gatz had great ambitions to rise above his poor, mundane background. He saw himself as a god-like figure who had great things to accomplish, and he believed that he could succeed. Working as a clam-digger and salmon-fisher on the shore of Lake Superior, his young imagination soared high with dreams of happiness and success.

He tried to better himself by going to college. But he gave up after two weeks. He returned to Lake Superior, and it was here that he met Dan Cody, a millionaire who had made his money from mining. He arrived one day in his yacht, and, impressed by the young James Gatz's intelligence and ambition, took him away. Working for Dan Cody for five years, the boy went three times round the American continent. When Dan Cody died, Gatz inherited a large sum of money but lost it all to Cody's girl friend in some legal proceedings. But the boy had gained in experience and he went on, on his own, to achieve the wealth and life of Jay Gatsby.

Nick's involvement with Gatsby, meanwhile, has come to a halt, after the meeting with Daisy. But he has become more and more intimate with Jordan.

One day he calls on Gatsby and, soon after his arrival, meets Tom, who has arrived with a couple of his friends. They have merely come to get a drink at Gatsby's. Tom and Mr Sloane are obviously contemptuous of Gatsby, but he is eager to know more of Tom. He tells Tom that he knows Daisy. When Mrs Sloane, to annoy her husband, invites Gatsby to dinner, he accepts readily, totally unaware that he is not really wanted. Tom becomes even more scornful of him. He and the Sloanes leave hastily while Gatsby goes off to fetch his car to accompany them.

Tom is a little disturbed by. Daisy's acquaintance with Gatsby. He comes with her to one of Gatsby's parties. Nick immediately feels a sense of unpleasantness at Tom's presence. Gatsby takes the Buchanans around. Soon, Tom and Daisy are separated; she dances with Gatsby while Tom goes off with another girl. Daisy is aware of Tom's movements and Nick observes that except for the time when she is alone with Gatsby, she has not enjoyed herself. Nick also watches the silly, meaningless behaviour of the other guests. He senses that Daisy is a little shocked and frightened by the crude gaiety and the empty lives of these people. But she does not really understand what she sees.

When Tom comes back to Nick and Daisy, he questions Gatsby's background. He is certain he is a bootlegger and is openly contemptuous of his newly-acquired wealth and his social gatherings. He voices his determination to find out more about the man. Daisy insists that Gatsby's money comes from a chain of drug-stores that he owns.

After Daisy has left them with Tom, Gatsby tells Nick of his anxieties. He is sure that Daisy has not enjoyed his party. He insists that she does not understand him or his desire. What he wants is that she should tell Tom that she has never loved him; as soon as she has done that, she and Gatsby can return to Louisville and get married from her house.

Nick tries to convince Gatsby that he cannot expect too much of Daisy, that he cannot repeat the past. Gatsby, however, scoffs at Nick and is sure that he can arrange everything just as it was five years ago. As he says this, Nick contemplates a moment five years ago when Gatsby must have felt that Daisy represented all that he desired of life. And thinking of Gatsby's ambition and absolute faith in life, Nick is faintly reminded of something, of some other situation which he cannot fully recall.

NOTES AND GLOSSARY:

the 'underground pipeline to Canada': there was a great deal of smuggling of illegal alcohol across the Great Lakes and the boundary with Canada. This was because Canada did not have Prohibition Laws which forbade the production and sale of liquor

his Platonic conception of himself. He was a Son of God—a phrase which, if it means anything, means just that—and he must be about His Father's business, the service of a vast, vulgar and meretricious beauty: Nick's description here sums up Gatsby's nature and ambition. According to the Greek philosopher, Plato, the ideal and the real are to be distinguished from each other. The ideal refers to the Perfect Forms or Ideas that exist in the spiritual world. Whatever physical or material object or form we have in our world, the real world, is a shadow or a representation of the Perfect or Ideal Form. What Nick is trying to say, therefore, is that Gatsby sees a perfect or ideal image of himself which rises over and above his physical reality as a poor clam-digger. As Nick sees it, this ideal image is also a god-like image. Gatsby must have seen himself as a Christ-like figure who must 'be about His Father's business'. The words are Jesus's reply to his mother when she finds Him in the Temple, talking to the elders. Gatsby's idealism, therefore, is a kind of religious dedication. At the end of Nick's description, however, there is a hint of anti-climax. Gatsby's dedication, his ideal, leads only to a vulgar kind of wealth and to Daisy

he could climb to it, if he climbed alone, and once there he could suck on the pap of life, gulp down the incomparable milk of wonder: from the very beginning Gatsby's relationship with Daisy has been built on fantasy

wed his unutterable visions to her perishable breath: the use of the word
'perishable' hints at Daisy's humanity. The descrip-
tion suggests the inevitable collapse of Gatsby's
dream because Daisy is human and can never come
up to Gatsby's ideal

Chapter VII

Gatsby's house is quiet now. He tells Nick that he wants privacy so that
Daisy's visits will not be talked about. One day, he informs Nick that
Daisy has invited them to lunch at her house. Nick feels that Gatsby is
planning to confront Tom at last.

The appointed day is broiling hot. Nick goes with Gatsby to Daisy's
house. Daisy overhears Tom on the telephone and feels sure he is
speaking to his mistress. Daisy then introduces Gatsby to her daughter
and Nick sees Gatsby looking quite startled. It is as if he has never
believed in the child's existence before. He becomes rather tense.

After lunch Tom sees Daisy and Gatsby looking at each other and
suddenly discovers that there is some secret intimacy between them.
Feeling angry and anxious, he agrees to the suggestion that they should
all go to town. When he decides to drive in Gatsby's car, Daisy goes
with Gatsby in Tom's car, leaving her husband to go with Nick and
Jordan.

Tom is irritable and expresses his contempt for Gatsby. He stops at
Wilson's garage for gas, telling Myrtle's husband that the car is his
latest buy. Then he learns from George that he and Myrtle are planning
to leave to go West. As they drive off, Nick catches a glimpse of Myrtle
at the window, looking at Jordan, evidently thinking she is Tom's wife.

Tom is in a panic now as he feels that he is about to lose both his wife
and his mistress. When they stop for drinks at the Plaza Hotel, he
quickly shows his hostility to Gatsby by questioning his background.
Then he forces Gatsby to tell him what is going on between him and
Daisy. When Gatsby gets Daisy to declare her love for him, Tom quickly
reminds her of some of their tender moments together. Daisy's feelings
for her husband are aroused, and she turns to Gatsby to say that she
had loved her husband once but that she had loved him too. Gatsby is
shattered by her words, even though she tells him that she now loves
only him. Tom, meanwhile, grows in confidence and defeats Gatsby's
last efforts to win Daisy over by exposing some of his rival's criminal
activities. Daisy is shocked, and, turning her back on Gatsby's appeal,
insists on going home. Feeling triumphant and sure of himself now,
Tom insists that Daisy travels with Gatsby in Gatsby's own car. The
two of them start off ahead of Tom, Nick and Jordan.

When the latter party arrives at Wilson's garage, they see signs of some disaster. They soon learn that Myrtle has been killed by a hit-and-run driver. From the description, Tom and the others know at once that Gatsby's yellow car was involved. When George Wilson sees Tom he gets very excited, and Tom has to tell him quickly that, although he has been driving the yellow car earlier, it does not belong to him.

On reaching Tom's house, Nick quickly takes leave of him and Jordan. He meets Gatsby, who has been waiting outside Tom's house, and learns that Daisy was driving the car when it hit Myrtle. But Gatsby intends to take the blame. He tells Nick that he will stay and watch all night over the Buchanan house, to make sure that Daisy is not bullied by her husband. When Nick takes a look into the house, he sees Tom and Daisy; they appear to him as if they were conspiring together.

NOTES AND GLOSSARY:

his career as Trimalchio: Gatsby is compared with a character from a Roman satire, *The Satyricon*, by Petronius (d.*c*.AD 65). Trimalchio was a wealthy man who held a sumptuous banquet for the people of Rome. The piece provided an occasion for the author's satirical attack on many leading figures of his time. At one point Fitzgerald considered calling his book *Trimalchio* because Gatsby's lavish parties and the social satire seem to parallel Petronius's work

commutation ticket: a season ticket

'I'm right across from you': Gatsby is eager to show Tom that he lives quite close to him. It seems as if he is trying to indicate that with the proximity of their houses, whatever social gap there is between them is narrowed. But Tom still treats Gatsby as a social inferior, as his behaviour in the rest of this chapter will show.

Ahead lay the scalloped ocean and the bounding blessed isles: 'the blessed isles' were the names of some mythical islands, so called because eternal peace was supposed to be found there. Nick's words show his desire for escape from the tension that is building up between Tom and Gatsby

'I'll take you in this circus wagon': this is Tom's scornful way of expressing contempt for Gatsby's vulgar, flashy possessions. Social snobbery is very much in evidence here

'I bought it last week': it is necessary that George should associate Gatsby's car with Tom. Even though Tom disclaims it after the accident, George Wilson still persists in seeking him out, and Tom is forced to save himself by identifying the car as Gatsby's.

Myrtle was peering down at the car: this explains Myrtle's behaviour just before she is killed. According to Gatsby, she had run towards the car as if she wanted to speak to someone she knew. She must have thought that Tom was still driving the car

elevated: the overhead railway of New York

Biloxi: significantly, Biloxi was an imposter. Tom evidently thinks that Gatsby is also one

Nowadays people begin by sneering at family life and family institutions: it is ironical that Tom should be so righteous about safeguarding family life. He has been unfaithful to Daisy right from the beginning of their marriage

Chapter VIII

That night Nick hardly sleeps at all. He is haunted by terrible dreams. When it is nearly dawn, he goes quickly to Gatsby's house, feeling a need to warn him about something.

He finds Gatsby, tired, depressed and alone. He informs Nick that nothing happened at Daisy's house. Nick stays with him and the house seems bigger than ever before. The atmosphere is gloomy and musty. The piano looks ghostly.

Nick tells Gatsby to go away from West Egg in case the police manage to trace his car. But Gatsby refuses to leave Daisy until he knows her plans. As they sit together Gatsby talks about his early life with Dan Cody, and tells Nick about his relationship with Daisy five years ago.

Gatsby had found Daisy exciting right from the beginning. She belonged to a social class which had always seemed remote from him. Even her house had an exciting air of mystery and gaiety about it. And, feeling aware of his own poverty and lack of background, he made the most of his time with Daisy. Gatsby pretended to her that he was financially secure and belonged to the same social class. He seduced her and although he had intended to leave the affair as it was, he became totally attached to Daisy—attached, that is, to her youth, her beauty and her wealth. And when they parted, the two of them were totally absorbed in each other.

Daisy was soon agitated by Gatsby's long absence. When he failed to return, she slowly turned back to her world of parties and orchids and was then quickly persuaded to make her life with Tom. Tom was muscular, powerful and rich.

Coming back to the present, Gatsby insists to Nick that Daisy has never loved Tom. But even if she has loved Tom for a while, this love is a small matter when compared to the grand, ideal kind of love between Daisy and himself.

At nine o'clock Nick sets off for his office. He is unwilling to leave Gatsby but manages to drag himself away. However, before he goes he tells Gatsby that he thinks him better than all the others put together.

At work, Nick feels restless and anxious. Jordan telephones him to say that she has left Daisy's house. When she voices her annoyance over Nick's careless departure the evening before, he becomes impatient at her lack of understanding.

Meanwhile, George Wilson is still bewailing the loss of his wife. He talks about finding the owner of the yellow car. He tells his friend Michaelis of his suspicions that his wife is involved in some affair and has been killed by her lover. Looking at Dr Eckleburg's eyes, George insists that God sees everything.

The next morning, Wilson is missing from his home. By two o'clock in the afternoon he is in West Egg, on the way to Gatsby's house.

Gatsby, meanwhile, is still waiting for Daisy to telephone him to tell him her plans. He goes to swim in the pool, while his butler waits by the telephone. Nick arrives back from work, just after the chauffeur hears the gun shots. They find Gatsby still lying on his mattress, floating on the water; Wilson's body is discovered a little way off in the grass.

NOTES AND GLOSSARY:

I heard a taxi go up Gatsby's drive: this indicates Gatsby's return from Daisy's house

a ghostly piano: the whole atmosphere in this chapter is gloomy and sinister and creates a sense of impending doom.

He wouldn't consider it: Gatsby's sentimentality is carried to extremes, to the point when he ignores all practical considerations. This is why Tom finds it so easy to take advantage of him

She was the first 'nice girl' he had ever known: this indicates that Gatsby is attracted to Daisy because of his desire for her kind of life. Gatsby's dream, therefore, is based on material interests after all. See *Commentary*, in the section under Theme (p.33) for an account of Gatsby's social struggles

Probably it had been tactful to leave Daisy's house, but the act annoyed me: Jordan is like Daisy, selfish and quick to abandon others to safeguard herself. Jordan's behaviour, therefore, parallels Daisy's desertion of Gatsby after Myrtle's accident

There was nothing in it but a small, expensive dog-leash: the significance of the incident with the dog in Chapter II becomes apparent here

Chapter IX

Amidst the threat of exaggerated newspaper reports, Nick is relieved that Gatsby's death is not made into a scandalous affair, linked to Myrtle's suspected adultery. Gatsby is pronounced to have been killed by a man maddened by grief over his wife's death.

Nick feels responsible for Gatsby now that he is dead, because no one else seems to care about him. As he arranges for the funeral, Nick tries to get people to attend, for so far no one has turned up at Gatsby's house. Tom and Daisy, however, have disappeared. Meyer Wolfshiem refuses to come even though Nick writes to ask him and even calls on him later to persuade him. Klipspringer phones, but only to ask for some shoes to be sent to him. When a call comes from Chicago Nick feels sure it is Daisy at last. But the caller is a man, who, evidently thinking that he is speaking to Gatsby, begins to tell him that one of his men has been arrested. Nick quickly interrupts and informs the speaker that Gatsby is dead. The caller breaks off immediately.

Then unexpectedly, Gatsby's father, Henry Gatz, arrives. And it is from him that Nick learns how rigidly Gatsby has worked towards self improvement from youth.

On the day of the funeral, there is one more unexpected guest. This is the man with the owl-eyed spectacles. And he voices Nick's contempt for the crowds of people who have been Gatsby's guests and who now keep away from his funeral.

Nick then recalls with longing his Mid-Western life. He remembers especially the traditions, the unchanging pattern of life and the close relationships. And Nick realises now that even when he was excited by life in the East he had been aware somehow that it was false and exaggerated. And after Gatsby's death, he becomes even more conscious of the decadence of the East. So Nick decides to leave, to return to his Mid-West. He goes to see Jordan before his departure. She accuses him of having been careless with her. Nick feels angry and sorry.

One afternoon he meets Tom in New York. Although Nick tries to avoid the meeting, Tom seems eager enough to greet him. Nick immediately condemns Tom for misleading Wilson and causing Gatsby's death. Tom, however, insists he had to protect himself from Wilson and he still thinks that Gatsby deserved to be shot. Nick's resentment against him remains, but he begins to understand that Tom and Daisy are selfish, irresponsible people who have no moral sense.

Nick pays a last visit to Gatsby's house before leaving the East. A little boy has scratched some abuse on the steps of the house. Nick quickly erases it. And as he stands there outside Gatsby's dark, lonely house, Nick realises that Gatsby's belief in life and love resembles the faith of the early sailors who had come to America, sure of happiness and success. And Nick realises too that Gatsby's imagination and hope is in all of us; like Gatsby then, we should strive after our dreams.

NOTES AND GLOSSARY:

a man 'deranged by grief': Nick is relieved that the tragedy of Gatsby's death (he dies for something of which he is not guilty) is not made worse by some false scandal about his 'affair' with Myrtle

'They picked him up when he handed the bonds over the counter': this is the only time when suspicions about Gatsby's criminal dealings are confirmed

James T. Hill: a businessman of the Mid-West, a friend of Fitzgerald's grandfather

'What I called up about was a pair of shoes I left there': Klipspringer's request at this time is not only thoughtless and tactless but also shows his utter lack of feeling for Gatsby

The rain poured down his thick glasses, and he took them off and wiped them': the eye image, seen in relation to Dr Eckleburg's eyes, points to the idea of defective vision—Gatsby's vision is totally influenced by imagination and ideals, and the Buchanans' is directed towards material interests only. (See *Commentary* in the section under Theme, for a detailed account, p.35). The action of Owl-eyes, in taking off his glasses and wiping them, is a further indication of the need to correct this faulty vision. Gatsby's death is directly related to his refusal to take a more practical view of life

a night scene by El Greco: Nick compares the presentation of slightly elongated figures in the paintings of the Spanish artist El Greco (1541–1614) with the distorted way of life in the East

Part 3

Commentary

BY THE TIME *The Great Gatsby* was completed in 1925, Fitzgerald had already written two best-selling novels, numerous short stories and several articles. These writings had earned him a certain popularity as a magazine writer and commentator of the contemporary scene—a popularity, however, which was to have an unfavourable effect on his reputation as a serious writer. For when *The Great Gatsby* was produced, critics, already familiar with his earlier works, were inclined to doubt its literary value. H.L. Mencken, one of the most prominent critics of the time, declared it to be 'no more than a glorified anecdote'.* And this kind of adverse opinion continued for the greater part of Fitzgerald's career. Only a few critics, and these mostly Fitzgerald's own close friends such as Edmund Wilson and John Peale Bishop, regarded his work seriously during his lifetime, but even they had to warn him continuously about the way he was wasting his talent in writing for magazines.

It was only in the 1940s after Fitzgerald's death that critics began to regard his work with more respect. This was partly due to the editorial work of Edmund Wilson, which had brought about the re-publication of such novels as *The Great Gatsby*, *The Last Tycoon* and several of Fitzgerald's best stories.

Theme

The success of *The Great Gatsby* lies partly in the fact that it can be read in different ways, so that it reaches out to a wide range of readers, from the ordinary man in the street to the scholar. To begin with, it is possible to read the novel simply as a love story where a rejected lover becomes wealthy, tries to win the lady back, and is abandoned by her at the end. The informal style seems to give the impression of an ordinary, simple plot.

On the other hand, the novel may be taken as a piece of social satire.†

*Quoted in *F. Scott Fitzgerald: a Collection of Critical Essays* ed. Arthur Mizener, Prentice-Hall, Englewood Cliffs, New Jersey, 1963, p.2.
†A satire is a piece of literature that ridicules people; it differs from comedy in that it aims to correct by ridicule, whereas comedy is meant merely to evoke laughter and amusement. Social satire ridicules the social behaviour and attitudes of a community.

On one level it comments on the careless gaiety and moral decadence of the period. The novel contains innumerable references to the contemporary scene. The wild extravagance of Gatsby's parties, the shallowness and aimlessness of the guests and the hint of Gatsby's involvement in crime all identify the period and the American setting. But as a piece of social commentary *The Great Gatsby* also describes the failure of the American dream, from the point of view that American political ideals conflict with the actual social conditions that exist.* For whereas American democracy is based on the idea of equality among people, the truth is that social discrimination still exists and the divisions among the classes cannot be overcome. Myrtle's attempt to break into the group to which the Buchanans belong is doomed to fail. Taking advantage of her vivacity, her lively nature, she seeks to escape from her own class. She enters into an affair with Tom and takes on his way of living. But she only becomes vulgar and corrupt like the rich. She scorns people from her own class and loses all sense of morality.† And for all her social ambition, Myrtle never succeeds in her attempt to find a place for herself in Tom's class. When it comes to a crisis, the rich stand together against all outsiders.

Myrtle's condition, of course, is a weaker reflection of Gatsby's more significant struggle. While Myrtle's desire springs from social ambition, Gatsby's is related more to his idealism, his faith in life's possibilities. Undoubtedly, his desire is also influenced by social considerations; Daisy, who is wealthy and beautiful, represents a way of life which is remote from Gatsby's and therefore more attractive because it is out of reach. However, social consciousness is not a basic cause. It merely directs and increases Gatsby's belief in life's possibilities. Like Myrtle, Gatsby struggles to fit himself into another social group, but his attempt is more urgent because his whole faith in life is involved in it. Failure, therefore, is more terrible for him. His whole career, his confidence in himself and in life is totally shattered when he fails to win Daisy. His death when it comes is almost insignificant, for, with the collapse of his dream, Gatsby is already spiritually dead.

As social satire, *The Great Gatsby* is also a comment on moral decadence in modern American society. The concern here is with the corruption of values and the decline of spiritual life—a condition which is ultimately related to the American Dream. For the novel recalls the early idealism of the first settlers. Fitzgerald himself relates Gatsby's dream to that of the early Americans for, at the end of the novel, Nick recalls the former Dutch sailors and compares their sense of wonder with Gatsby's hope. The book also seems to investigate how Americans

*See Part 1, The American Dream, p.11.
†See A.E. Dyson, '*The Great Gatsby:* Thirty years after' in *F. Scott Fitzgerald: a Collection of Critical Essays* ed. Mizener, pp.112–124.

lost their spiritual purpose as material success wiped out spiritual goals. The lives of the Buchanans, therefore, filled with material comforts and luxuries, and empty of purpose, represents this condition. Daisy's lament is especially indicative of this:

'What'll we do with ourselves this afternoon?' cried Daisy, 'and the day after that, and the next thirty years?' (p.102).

Fitzgerald stresses the need for hope and dreams to give meaning and purpose to man's efforts. Striving towards some ideal is the way by which man can feel a sense of involvement, a sense of his own identity. Certainly, Gatsby, with 'his extraordinary gift of hope' (p.6), set against the empty existence of Tom and Daisy, seems to achieve a heroic greatness. As Nick himself declares:

If personality is an unbroken series of successful gestures, then there was something gorgeous about him, some heightened sensitivity to the promises of life, as if he were related to one of those intricate machines that register earthquakes ten thousand miles away. (p.6)

Nick's approval of Gatsby is made clearer when he says: 'They're a rotten crowd . . . You're worth the whole damn bunch put together.' (p.133)

But Fitzgerald goes on to state that the failure of hopes and dreams, the failure of the American Dream itself, is unavoidable, not only because reality cannot keep up with ideals, but also because the ideals are in any case usually too fantastic to be realised. The heroic presentation of Gatsby, therefore, should not be taken at face value, for we cannot overlook the fact that Gatsby is naive, impractical and over-sentimental. It is this which makes him attempt the impossible, to repeat the past. There is something pitiful and absurd about the way he refuses to grow up. Nick's words indicate this when he tells of his conversation with Gatsby:

'Can't repeat the past?' he cried incredulously. 'Why of course you can!'
He looked around him wildly, as if the past were lurking here in the shadow of his house, just out of reach of his hand.
'I'm going to fix everything just the way it was before,' he said, nodding determinedly. 'She'll see.' (p.96)

What Fitzgerald does, therefore, is not merely to show Gatsby's heroic imagination against Tom's and Daisy's materialism; through the contrast between the two ways of life, Gatsby's and the Buchanans', Fitzgerald asserts the idea that man needs to combine imagination and material values. On the one hand, there are people like Tom and Daisy and their set, who cannot see beyond the material and the physical. On the other, there is Gatsby, whose faith cuts him off totally from the rational and the practical. One way of life is as unhealthy as the other. The image of Dr Eckleburg's gigantic eyes, overlooking the valley of ashes, therefore, is not only an ironic indication of the love for worldly things in Daisy's world. This image of the eyes is also a comment on faulty vision—short-sightedness on the one hand, and long-sightedness on the other. One cannot see beyond the immediate and the superficial; the other cannot see the material, practical aspects, only the dream.

Seen in this way, Gatsby is juxtaposed against Tom and Daisy. But they are similar in one respect. Both are extremely self-centred, in that they are only occupied with their own interests. Gatsby's self-centredness, however, is more purposeful and has more significance because it stems from his idealism. The Buchanans' is destructive and ruthless because it leads to irresponsibility and thoughtlessness. Therefore, if Nick seems to approve of Gatsby more than of the others, this is merely because he prefers the imaginative life to the material life. Nick's attitude by no means indicates that Gatsby's fantasy, as it stands, is all good.

Since the materialistic and the imaginative aspects of life are juxtaposed and identified separately with the two groups, the confrontation or clash between them is the result of their conflicting values. Gatsby, more heroic and magnificent because of his idealism, is also more helpless against the worldliness of the Buchanans. His ultimate disappointment is all the more shattering because Daisy Buchanan is the object of his dream. The failure of this dream is an experience from which he can never recover since the dream has become the centre of his life. And when the dream fails, Gatsby's 'Platonic conception of himself' (p.86), his whole belief in himself and in life crumbles too. His death is the only possible and logical consequence.

Fitzgerald's comment on the failure of Gatsby's dream is also a statement on the failure of the American Dream. And from here his account broadens to a general description of man's condition. The juxtaposition of the materialistic and imaginative attitudes significantly indicates a moving away from faith and hope in a world where material interests have driven out sentimentality and faith. What is more, imagination, even if it persists, is utterly helpless and defenceless against a material society. It can only be defeated. Gatsby's fate does not remain his alone. What happens to Gatsby is a warning for the rest of mankind.

Structure and technique

The structure of the novel is naturally related to the theme. And as the theme, as has been established, concerns the opposing attitudes and values of two groups of people, namely the Buchanans and Gatsby, the narrative arrangement must necessarily alternate, that is move from one to the other until the two groups meet. This two way movement of the narrative is controlled by the actor/observer who is actually reviewing the action after a certain lapse of time. His maturity, newly-achieved as a result of his experience with the two sets of characters, helps to maintain a balance between the two kinds of extreme behaviour identified with the two groups. Operating above this is the recurrence of images, motifs and the unstated but implied connections between characters and events.

One striking fact about the novel's design is the way in which the chapter divisions neatly provide the structural framework for the narrative. From Chapters I to IV the juxtaposition of the two sets of characters is effectively achieved so that the contrasts (and similarities) between them are consistently maintained. And from Chapters V to IX the action advances steadily and with mounting momentum towards a climax and resolution. Each chapter, containing one or two significant episodes, urges the plot forward another step towards the ultimate tragedy.

Chapter I, the first of the four chapters given to the descriptions of the main characters, points at once to the conflicting attitudes of the two groups. It also establishes the fact that both are similarly self-centred. This dramatic introduction of the two groups of characters comes just after the presentation of the actor/observer, Nick Carraway. Nick asserts that it is a habit with him to be tolerant and to reserve judgement. With Gatsby, however, Nick's detachment gives way to admiration and respect. For, although Gatsby stands for everything that Nick scorns, his 'extraordinary gift for hope' (p.6), his idealism, is so immense that there is something magnificent about it.

The fact that Nick clarifies the time that occurs between his narration and the actual events that occurred is significant, because this also indicates that the interval has helped him to review the events and so understand them better. With this new understanding, Nick's comments on Gatsby's idealism and on 'the foul dust that floated in the wake of his dreams' (p.6) at once influence the reader to regard Gatsby with sympathy and expectation.

The story proper commences after this with a description of Nick's family and traditional Mid-Western background and his anticipation of a more exciting life in the East:

> And so with the sunshine and the great bursts of leaves growing on the trees, just as things grow in fast movies, I had that familiar conviction that life was beginning over again with the summer. (p.7)

Significantly, and in keeping with his Mid-Western background which he has just related, Nick's feeling that he is 'a guide, a pathfinder, an original settler' (p.7) seems to announce his hopeful, optimistic outlook. This in turn seems to echo Gatsby's idealistic view of life, so that Nick already appears to share a certain similar hopeful attitude with Gatsby.

Ironically, it is just after this moment of anticipation that Nick meets the Buchanans. Immediately, the description shows up their life of physical and material enjoyment. For Tom and Daisy are striking with their physical appeal—he so muscular and powerful, and she so radiant and glowing. And they live a life of wealth, with their red and white Georgian Colonial mansion, its sunken Italian garden and other signs of wealth. Against this elaborate setting, however, the atmosphere is superficial and hollow. Nick finds himself participating in a conversation which is aimless and meaningless. He writes:

> I told her how I had stopped off in Chicago for a day on my way East, and how a dozen people had sent their love through me.
> 'Do they miss me?' she cried ecstatically.
> 'The whole town is desolate. All the cars have the left rear wheel painted black as a mourning wreath, and there's a persistent wail all night along the north shore.'
> 'How gorgeous! Let's go back, Tom. Tomorrow!' (p.12)

The lack of purpose, 'the absence of all desire' (p.14) is a sharp contrast to Nick's own ambitiousness and his sense of anticipation in coming to the East. Furthermore, the shallowness of the Buchanans is immediately contrasted with Gatsby's intense feelings. On coming home from the Buchanans' house, Nick sees his neighbour standing alone in the night, his hands reaching out longingly for a green light across the bay.

> But I didn't call to him, for he gave a sudden intimation that he was content to be alone—he stretched out his arms towards the dark water in a curious way, and, far as I was from him, I could have sworn he was trembling. (pp.21-22)

Very quickly then, the first chapter has introduced the narrator and has also presented the opposing sets of characters and their essential qualities. The alternating movement of the narrative, first towards one group and then towards the other, which will continue in the next three chapters, is also established.

The progression from Chapter I to Chapter II is marked by the two-way flow of the narrative. Whereas Chapter I ends dramatically with the brief view of Gatsby in his moment of yearning, Chapter II opens with the swing back to the other side, that to which Tom and Daisy belong. The valley of ashes symbolises the empty existence of the New Yorkers.

> About half way between West Egg and New York the motor road hastily joins the railroad and runs beside it for a quarter of a mile, so

as to shrink away from a certain desolate area of land. This is the valley of ashes—a fantastic farm where ashes grow like wheat into ridges and hills and grotesque gardens; where ashes take the forms of houses and chimneys and rising smoke and, finally, with transcendent effort, of ash-grey men. . . . (p.23)

Appropriately, this chapter goes on to a description of Tom's affair with Myrtle. The account also covers another aspect of Tom's life—his love affair as opposed to his domestic life already projected in Chapter I. The two areas of activities establish more effectively the evidence of moral carelessness among the rich. But more than this, the narrative turns now to the description of characters belonging to the lower middle class. Myrtle, Catherine and the McKees belong to this group. Their manners and attitudes, however, show the same restlessness and idleness that Tom and Daisy represent. If Myrtle and her crowd are more vulgar and their manners more artificial, this is merely because they are less sure of themselves. But basically their false values are influenced by those of the rich whom they try so desperately to imitate. So Myrtle's concern with social distinction and status even in marriage is an echo of Tom's racial and class consciousness. Compare Myrtle's views with Tom's: Myrtle says

'I married him because I thought he was a gentleman,' she said finally. 'I thought he knew something about breeding, but he wasn't fit to lick my shoe.' (p.33)

and Tom says

'. . . It's up to us, who are the dominant race, to watch out or these other races will have control of things.' (p.15)

And what is more, Myrtle's crude attempts to introduce Nick to her sister Catherine are reminders of Daisy's plans to have Nick and Jordan together. And the McKees' efforts to talk intelligently about photography ironically parallels Tom's desire to sound scholarly:

'This idea is that we're Nordics. . . . And we've produced all the things that go to make civilisation—oh, science and art, and all that. Do you see?' (p.15)

The artificiality and shallowness of Myrtle and her friends, therefore, fit in with the picture of superficiality already associated with the Buchanans and their set. The way of life identified with the rich is thus seen to embrace the New Yorkers in general, from the lower to the higher social ranks. The drunken scene at the end of the chapter completes the prevailing mood of careless gaiety and indulgence. Ominously,

Nick is also drunk, an indication that he too is easily influenced by the decadent way of life in the East. For Nick himself has earlier, in this same chapter, re-asserted that he is both attracted to and repulsed by life in New York: 'I was within and without, simultaneously enchanted and repelled by the inexhaustible variety of life.' (p.33)

As later events will show, Nick does move towards this easy life of lazy enjoyment as he finds himself attracted to Jordan. But with his growing involvement with Gatsby, Nick is forced out of his passiveness. He becomes sympathetic to and concerned about Gatsby's idealism.

Contrasted with Chapter II and the extended portrayal of careless living, Chapter III focuses on Gatsby. Though his parties apparently contain the same kind of decadence, they are actually the means to an end, Daisy. Accordingly, we see in the midst of this hollow gaiety, Gatsby standing alone, growing 'more correct as the fraternal hilarity' (p.45) increases. So that while the whole anarchic scene at Gatsby's house shows up the wild behaviour of the New Yorkers, it also illuminates Gatsby's dignity and contrasting air of discipline.

The chapter looks forward to later tragic developments. The incident where Nick, wandering around at Gatsby's party, mistakes the host for a guest, does not merely contribute to the idea of faulty vision which characterises the two groups of characters. This incident of mistaken identity comes before the scene where Owl-eyes is wrongly accused of driving the car that lands in a ditch. The two incidents together forebodingly anticipate the later tragedy, when Gatsby is falsely identified as the driver of the car that kills Myrtle. Indeed, the chapter contains two incidents of careless driving, because the occasion when Jordan nearly knocks down a man is also described here. All this prepares the reader for the final accident which will have far more terrible consequences.

Nick's account of his work and life in New York provides his narrative with a necessary break. The interval helps to reassert the distance of the action from the reader by reminding him of the presence of the narrator. This distance in turn helps the reader to view the action as a whole, that is to see the two groups of characters in relation to one another. What is important is the overall effect of the action, not single events or a single line of action. At the same time, the pause that is created throws into relief the fast pace at which the Buchanans and Gatsby live. After the heady way these two groups live, the slowing down of the action here helps the reader to take a breath, as it were, by allowing him to return momentarily to the world of ordinary action and routine that is Nick's world. Apart from George Wilson, Nick is the only character in the novel who is soberly occupied with work. This fact alone reassures the reader that Nick, unlike the others, belongs to the daily world of normal, uncomplicated routine.

As for Nick's response to New York, the account here describes how his sense of expectation and excitement continues: 'I began to like New York, the racy, adventurous feel of it at night, and the satisfaction that the constant flicker of men and women and machines gives to the restless eye.' (p.51)

Nick has as yet not become involved with Gatsby or the Buchanans although he has begun to move in their circles. So his confidence is still unshaken. But he has become more intimate with Jordan, though not fully involved. Significantly, his description of Jordan's cheating ways is an anticipation of Daisy's irresponsibility. His lack of concern about 'dishonesty in a woman' (p.52) is, therefore, ironically foolish. Stemming from his manly pride, his attitude will eventually give way to a horrifying realisation of the destructive nature of this 'female' weakness. The account of the near accident in which Jordan is involved, gruesomely anticipating Daisy's reckless driving, hints at the sheer carelessness of these people which Nick has yet to perceive. For he still does not understand that deceitfulness and irresponsibility such as that of which Jordan is guilty, actually represent the attitude of a whole society, that to which Jordan, Tom and Daisy belong. For the moment, Nick is only aware that he is attracted by Jordan. And, smiling at Jordan's female weakness and folly, Nick considers his own honesty with much satisfaction: 'Everyone suspects himself of at least one of the cardinal virtues, and this is mine: I am one of the few honest people that I have ever known.' (p.53)

After the break created by Nick's account of his own activities, the pace picks up again at the beginning of Chapter IV as the narrator returns to the description of Gatsby's affairs. The opening passage, written in a vivid, racy style, continues the depiction of Gatsby's way of life, seen in its public aspect, from the point of view of his social activities and his popular image. But this public life shows the quality of the people who descend upon Gatsby rather than revealing the personality of the host. The chapter then goes on to describe Gatsby's private world, seen in terms of his personal relationships and activities. Gatsby displays an obvious restlessness which recalls that of the Buchanans and their crowd. As Nick observes, 'He was never quite still; there was always a tapping foot somewhere or the impatient opening and closing of a hand' (p.56). This brings to mind Tom's and Daisy's ceaseless chatter and nervous pursuit of action. But Gatsby's restlessness is of a different kind. It relates to a certain purposefulness in the man. This explains his determination here to tell Nick about himself:

'I'm going to make a big request of you today,' he said . . . 'so I thought you ought to know something about me. . . .' (p.59)

Gatsby's private life is as colourful and as spectacular as his public activities. His description of his Oxford education, his travels, and his participation in the war, leaves Nick utterly fascinated, and he says, 'My incredulity was submerged in fascination now; it was like skimming hastily through a dozen magazines.' (p.58)

Besides this, the account of Gatsby's neat though corrupt dismissal of the policeman who stops him for speeding, and Nick's observation of the meeting with Wolfshiem also increase the atmosphere of mystery and power that surrounds Gatsby. Ironically, the image of authority that Gatsby presents at this point will be replaced by his utter helplessness in the succeeding chapter as he nervously waits for Daisy at Nick's house. On top of this, the ultimate destruction of Gatsby by the Buchanans ironically contrasts with the strength and power which he shows here.

With the double view given of Gatsby's private world, that is, mysteriously authoritative and confident on the one hand and tragically helpless on the other, it is appropriate that the account here contains a passage that reflects the idea of hope and defeat. As Nick drives with Gatsby to New York, they come to a point where they see the city 'in its first wild promise of all the mystery and the beauty in the world' (p.60). And just after this they see a funeral procession: 'A dead man passed us in a hearse heaped with blooms, followed by two carriages with drawn blinds. . . .' (p.60) The ironic descriptions of life and death, of promise and defeat, is particularly ominous at this point, when Gatsby is about to meet Daisy again and have his desire fulfilled.

Gatsby's love affair with Daisy five years ago, coming to the reader through two narrators and therefore placed at a further distance away, seems more unreal and even more fantastic. Gatsby's attempt to re-enact the past must seem totally foolish and absurd. Moreover, Jordan's cynical tone, when she describes Daisy's inconsistent behaviour, mocks at Gatsby and his dream. The children's song which succeeds this is an apt criticism of Gatsby's immense ambition:

'I'm the Sheik of Araby.
Your love belongs to me.
At night when you're asleep
Into your tent I'll creep—' (p.68)

And yet, seen against a society corrupted by money and idleness represented here by Wolfshiem and the Buchanans, Gatsby's sentimentality contains a certain magnificence and beauty. Unlike Wolfshiem, who gambles to make more money, Gatsby gambles for love. He plays for higher stakes, and, when he loses, he loses everything, his faith, his life. At his earlier meeting with Wolfshiem, Gatsby's desire has already been hinted at. Wolfshiem recalls former days at the Metropole and this anticipates the later account of Gatsby's desire for his past. But unlike

Gatsby's persistence, Wolfshiem very quickly leaves aside the memories to get down to business. His presumption that Nick is a business connection, however, like the car accident at Gatsby's house described in the previous chapter, adds to the theme of mistaken identity and looks forward to the subsequent event of Gatsby's tragic end.

So much then for the first four chapters, which have served to establish the two groups of characters and their ways of life. Although the narration has followed an alternating pattern, swinging from one group to the other, moving from one aspect of a person's life to another, the overall arrangement is to divide the first four chapters equally between the Buchanans and Gatsby. The first two chapters project the domestic and extra-marital life of Tom Buchanan. The third and fourth chapters vividly present the public and private aspects of Gatsby's personality. In Chapter IV, however, the action has progressed with the account of Gatsby's arrangements to meet Daisy again. Now, in Chapter V the climax is reached. The reunion with Daisy occurs at last. With this, the two groups of characters and their lines of action become entangled. Subsequent events in the later chapters are merely developments resulting from this point of entanglement.

The meeting between Gatsby and Daisy is ironically comical. Gatsby, seen first in his condition of utter nervousness and anxiety, and then in his state of dazed happiness, is almost absurd. Daisy, however, seems to show little of the turbulence that Gatsby is going through. When she arrives, unaware of what is in store, she is childishly excited and gay at the prospect of a secret assignation with Nick. And when she does meet Gatsby, the only sign of her confusion is her artificial voice, and even this is temporary. She soon recovers, and when she next speaks her voice is 'as matter-of-fact as it could ever be' (p.76). Ironically and ominously, then, Daisy does not seem to share Gatsby's emotional intensity. She sheds some tears, but this could easily be an affected reaction to Gatsby's obvious feelings.

Whatever the case, this meeting with Daisy must bring some disenchantment for Gatsby. Daisy herself in person can hardly measure up to the idealised image that Gatsby must have built up in his mind for his dream is utterly fantastic. As Nick says:

> It had gone beyond her, beyond everything. He had thrown himself into it with a creative passion, adding to it all the time, decking it out with every bright feather that drifted his way. No amount of fire or freshness can challenge what a man can store up in his ghostly heart. (p.83)

Of course, Daisy herself is childish and flighty. Her excited response to Gatsby's house and clothes are further indications of her shallowness. Klipspringer's song, coming at this point, reminds the reader of the harsh reality of Daisy's moneyed world—a world which will eventually shatter Gatsby's dream:

> In the morning,
> In the evening,
> Ain't we got fun—
> One thing's sure and nothing's surer
> The rich get richer and the poor get—children.
> In the meantime.
> In between time—(p.83)

Gatsby's vulgar display of his wealth and possessions, therefore, seem to be an unconscious response to Daisy's materialistic values.

The undertone of harsh reality that cuts through Gatsby's fantasy in this chapter is further increased by the events which link with later tragic developments. For one thing, there is the opening scene that shows Gatsby's house most brightly lit up for the last time, seeming to bring Gatsby's own condition of celebration and hope to a climax now that he is about to meet Daisy again. This scene contrasts ironically with the desolation that finally surrounds the place after Gatsby's death:

> Gatsby's house was still empty when I left—the grass on the lawn had grown as long as mine. (p.155)

The event of Gatsby anxiously waiting for Daisy to come to tea at Nick's house ominously foreshadows the day when, after Myrtle's death, Gatsby waits for Daisy to call and is found by George Wilson. As one critic has observed, Gatsby's words to Nick here in Chapter V as he voices his impatience are ironically relevant.* He says to Nick: 'Nobody's coming to tea. It's too late!' (p.74) It is indeed too late, five years too late, for him. Gatsby's later insistence, therefore, that it is possible to repeat the past, must seem ironical and futile.

For Gatsby, however, the realisation of his dream must seem close with his meeting with Daisy again. This desire to revive his relationship with Daisy is to be seen as part of Gatsby's grand idealistic plan. It is a plan on which his whole personality and career are established. Therefore, the subsequent account in Chapter VI narrates the change of young James Gatz into Jay Gatsby. According to Nick, the name and life of Gatsby are built around the god-like image which the young James Gatz had of himself; his love for Daisy is similarly based on this ideal. But if his whole identity and personality rest on hope and ideals, how defenceless must he be in a materialistic society, and how disastrous will be the disappointment when it comes. The reunion with Daisy,

*Richard D. Lehan, *F. Scott Fitzgerald and the Craft of Fiction*, Southern Illinois University Press, Carbondale, 1972, p.118.

therefore, is even more significant now, as it becomes obvious that if Daisy fails to live up to Gatsby's expectations, she will probably destroy the confidence and faith upon which his identity and life are established. Gatsby's disenchantment with Daisy, however, seems certain as the encounter with Tom and Mr and Mrs Sloane emphasises the carelessness and thoughtlessness of Daisy's world. Tom, for one, seems determined to break down the mystery surrounding Gatsby's background and life:

> 'I'd like to know who he is and what he does,' insisted Tom. 'And I think I'll make a point of finding out.' (p.94)

The meeting with Tom and the arrival of the Buchanans at one of Gatsby's parties, therefore, threaten to destroy the idealism of Gatsby's world. As Nick himself observes, Tom's presence brings a 'peculiar quality of oppressiveness' (p.90). He goes on to state that he has 'felt an unpleasantness in the air, a pervading harshness that hadn't been there before.' (p.91)

The sense of unease increases with Nick's remark that the promise that Daisy holds for Gatsby may be an empty one after all. For Daisy has a natural gift for stirring hope and desire. As Nick listens to her singing here, her voice contains a magic which, however, is only superficial:

> Daisy began to sing with the music in a husky, rhythmic whisper, bringing out a meaning in each word that it had never had before and would never have again. (p.94)

But Gatsby's imagination is given totally to the worship of Daisy. His desire to talk about her and of their love indicates this:

> He knew that when he kissed this girl, and forever wed his unutterable visions to her perishable breath, his mind would never romp again like the mind of God. (p.96)

And the chapter ends on this note of uncertainty, where Gatsby's hope is seen against Tom's hardness, on the one hand, and Daisy's shallowness, on the other. But Gatsby's large imagination stirs a certain response in Nick, as he is reminded vaguely of something familiar. Only in the last chapter does Nick realise that Gatsby's dream recalls the hope and idealism of the early American settlers.

Chapter VII continues to trace the development of events but here the action reaches a peak as incidents drive the characters to a final point of confrontation. The chapter opens quietly enough with Nick's reference to Gatsby's changed way of life since he has met Daisy again. In order that he can meet Daisy privately, Gatsby keeps his house quiet and gives no more parties. This change also indicates his readiness for a totally new life with Daisy, a life of perfect love and happiness. Ironically, however, Gatsby's expectations are soon to be shattered.

It is at Daisy's lunch that things begin to happen. Nick senses that Gatsby and Daisy are planning to confront Tom during lunch. There is a growing sense of desperation among the characters, namely Gatsby and the Buchanans. There is Daisy, a little nervous and confused to have her lover and husband lunching together at her house:

> 'But it's so hot,' insisted Daisy, on the verge of tears, 'and everything's so confused. Let's all go to town!' (p.102)

There is also Gatsby, who is caught in a feeling of uneasiness as he meets Daisy's daughter for the first time. The child, after all, is the first solid symbol of Daisy's marriage, and indicates a certain bond between Daisy and Tom which is undeniable. As Nick observes: 'Afterwards he kept looking at the child with surprise. I don't think he had ever really believed in its existence before.' (p.101)

Finally there is Tom, confused at the sudden discovery that there is some secret relationship between his wife and Gatsby. Then he learns that Myrtle may be leaving him.

The climax, when it comes, shows Tom in control of the situation. Although he fumbles a little at the beginning when Gatsby informs him that Daisy has never loved him, he soon recovers. Then, in his calculating way, he takes advantage of the fact that Gatsby has been separated from Daisy for five years and that Daisy's feelings can be easily aroused. By recalling their happier days together, he makes Daisy admit that she has loved him. When she tells Gatsby that she has loved him too, the use of the word 'too' shows clearly that her feelings for him come after her love for Tom. For Gatsby, who has had dreams of a perfect love, what Daisy is offering is a bitter disappointment. Any further attempt to win Daisy, however, fails when Tom cleverly frightens her with the information that Gatsby is involved in criminal activities. Gatsby is quite helpless against Tom's ruthless tactics. The worst, however, is not over. When the group sets off for home from the Plaza Hotel, a bigger crisis awaits them.

The narrative shifts to Wilson and slowly builds up to the horrible accident in which Myrtle is killed. The direct account conveys the violent and shocking event immediately, thus adding to the drama and suspense. Tom's assumption that Gatsby was driving the car in which he and Daisy were driving at the time of the accident increases the anxiety. When Nick talks to Gatsby at last and discovers that Daisy was in fact the driver, the reader feels a sense of relief. For all this while, won by Gatsby's earnestness and sincere desire, the reader's sympathy has unconsciously moved towards him. But it is only here, as he feels lightened by the knowledge of Gatsby's innocence, that the reader becomes conscious of his own attachment. And yet the anxiety is not immediately lifted. Gatsby declares his desire to shield Daisy. The chapter ends uncertainly, awaiting the final move from Tom and Daisy concerning the accident and Gatsby's fate.

On the whole, the climactic action in this chapter comes through by way of a quickening of the pace of the narrative. This is achieved by means of the rapid movements of the characters as the point of confrontation is reached. The group of characters, comprising Gatsby, Daisy, Tom, Nick and Jordan, moves restlessly from one place to another, from Daisy's house to Wilson's garage to the Plaza Hotel, then back to Wilson's garage and home. The heat, too, that pervades in the earlier part of the chapter contributes to the oppressive sense of strain.

Chapter VIII opens in an atmosphere of impending doom. There is Nick with his 'savage, frightening dreams' (p.127) and the feeling that he has to warn Gatsby about something. Even as he listens to Gatsby's recollection of his early relationship with Daisy, Nick notes the hint of shadows that mars the flowering of a new day:

> It was dawn now on Long Island and we went about opening the rest of the windows downstairs, filling the house with grey-turning, gold-turning light. The shadow of a tree fell abruptly across the dew and ghostly birds began to sing among the blue leaves. (p.131)

To add to this, there is Nick's own strange reluctance to go to the city. He misses one train after another:

> I didn't want to go to the city . . . I didn't want to leave Gatsby. I missed that train, and then another, before I could get myself away. (p.132)

Even at his office, his anxiety is evident in the way he starts up at the sound of the phone, as if fearful of bad news.

The narrative structure in this chapter also helps to build up the atmosphere of impending doom. The narrative moves forward and backward frequently, creating a sense of confusion and disorder that contributes to the unease and anxiety.

In the early part of this chapter, Nick describes his eagerness to meet Gatsby after his night of nightmares and dreams. At their meeting Gatsby starts to recall his early relationship with Daisy, minutely describing their meeting and their growing involvement with each other. It is as if Gatsby is trying to cling on to some hope that Daisy will not let him down in the end. In between Gatsby's recollections, however, the account breaks off to refer back to the present—the ghostly morning and Nick's growing anxiety.

More significantly, however, the shifts from past to present and back again, are accompanied by a sense of time passing, from before dawn to dawn and then to nine o'clock when Nick goes to work. And the concern with time continues. At his office, Nick repeatedly asserts the day's progress to noon, 'Just before noon the phone woke me, and I started up with sweat breaking out on my forehead' (p.133). And then he says, 'I called Gatsby's house a few minutes later, but the line was busy. . . . It was just noon.' (p.134)

Apart from this, the hour by hour recording of George Wilson's movements that day, and the timing of Gatsby's activities that afternoon, is significant, because a sense of urgency and an expectation of disaster increases throughout the chapter.

The event of Nick's conversation with Jordan Baker on the phone emphasises for the last time the distorted values of Daisy's world, because Jordan and Daisy share the same kind of irresponsibility and carelessness. Jordan abandons Daisy after the accident just as Daisy herself deserts Gatsby. Jordan tells Nick of her departure from the Buchanan house. Unconcerned about the accident, she only thinks of Nick's careless goodbye to her the night before. Nick, however, is not very interested. He is only concerned about Gatsby now.

The account of Wilson's and Gatsby's movements that afternoon avoids a direct description of the killing. The tragic event is related through Nick's discovery when he reaches Gatsby's house later that day. This indirectness holds the suspense right to the end but it also creates an atmosphere of tragic unreality.

In Chapter IX the account rounds up the action with a description of Nick's preparations for Gatsby's burial. Reasserting the time distance between Nick and the events in East and West Egg, the chapter juxtaposes the two main groups of characters for the last time. There is Gatsby, vulnerable to the very end, even after his death, when he is abandoned by everyone; and there are the New Yorkers, the Buchanans, Meyer Wolfshiem and so on, whose uncaring disregard for duty and obligation has defeated Gatsby and who, even at his death, deny him a last act of kindness and consideration.

Nick's sympathy for Gatsby increases his hostility towards the uncaring world. His feeling for Gatsby also arouses a sense of responsibility towards him. And so he takes on the preparations for the funeral and even tries to persuade people to attend.

Wolfshiem's account of Gatsby's poor beginnings and Henry Gatz's revelation of his son's 'work schedule' (his personal timetable) show just how much Gatsby has worked to achieve his ambition. He has come a long way from his poverty-stricken days, by means of faith, determination and hard work. And so his death is all the more tragic and wasteful. But he has lived by a distorted vision of life. Owl-eyes' rubbing his spectacles as he stands beside the grave seems to indicate Gatsby's need to correct his faulty outlook.

Nick's encounter with Jordan and Tom at this point not only rounds up the action but completes Nick's own development as a character. The meeting with Jordan, and her annoyance over Nick's careless behaviour towards her, confirms for him that Jordan, like the rest of Daisy's friends, is just as self-centred and unfeeling. But Nick is made to realise that from Jordan's point of view, his careless dismissal of her has seemed cruel. The knowledge that he needs to see things from another's viewpoint brings a feeling of anger at himself and his own ignorance.

Nick's encounter with Tom leads to a greater sense of tolerance and understanding. For when Tom insists that his betrayal of Gatsby to George Wilson was necessary, Nick begins to accept the fact that the action, in Tom's eyes, is highly justified. It is all a question of values which Tom himself cannot help. And Nick, with his new knowledge, says: 'I shook hands with him; it seemed silly not to for I felt suddenly as though I were talking to a child' (pp.154–5). But in spite of this new tolerance, Nick returns to his Middle Western life. Repulsed by the East and the way in which worldly life corrupts and distorts man's values and behaviour, Nick regards his provincial background with greater respect and appreciation. But he holds on to the memory of Gatsby and his idealism. His last moments in New York are marked by his return to Gatsby's house. His final tribute to Gatsby is his realisation that Gatsby's idealism, although fantastic, relates to a deep need in mankind—the need for faith and hope.

In our discussion of the chapter arrangement, the organisation of events and the direction of the narrative, we have seen on several occasions how the use of the narrator allows for an ordering of events which does not follow the time sequence. The use of such flash-backs helps to place events at their most effective and relevant positions in the narrative, either for emphasis, or for ironical comment or juxtaposition. But more than this, the use of a narrator with a foreknowledge of the outcome of events is a help towards creating in the reader a suitable frame of mind right at the beginning of the novel. In the first part of Chapter I Nick informs his readers beforehand how he is drawn from his detachment to become awed and impressed by Gatsby. This early statement of his final involvement with, and approval of, Gatsby's 'gift for hope' (p.6) at once directs the reader's interest and expectations towards Gatsby, even before he appears. Therefore when Daisy and Tom are introduced, our judgement, using Gatsby as a point of comparison and reference, will immediately find them different. The reader's response is, therefore, swift, and his attention more alert. Foreknowledge arouses anticipation, and the reader's interest throughout this early part of the novel is caught up with the expectation of Nick's progress towards Gatsby.

The two groups of characters being what they are, extremely imaginative on the one hand, and extremely materialistic on the other, the success of the book depends on the assertion of a central in-between character—one who is practical and sensible as well as sensitive and imaginative. Nick Carraway, the narrator, embodies this middle position very suitably with his commonsense, his purposeful, hopeful outlook and his warmth. Indeed Nick is a combination of practical efficiency and sensitivity. Like Gatsby, he is also from the Mid-West, but he has grown up with the optimism *and* the material practicality typical of the people of the area. And so, while Nick is able to admire and sympathise with Gatsby's immense faith in life, he is also quick to warn him not to expect too much of Daisy, that he cannot repeat the past.

The intrusion of the narrator between the reader and the characters of the novel is to establish a distance between the latter two. The novel is concerned with the need to balance imagination with practical sensibleness; it is undesirable for the reader to identify himself entirely with Gatsby, and this he might be likely to do without the presence of the narrator. Nick being there, however, the reader identifies with him and thus achieves a more balanced view of Gatsby, who is seen as opposed to Daisy and Tom.

Imagery

The imagery in *The Great Gatsby* follows the juxtaposition of the two ways of life represented by Gatsby and by the Buchanans. Images of light and darkness, for example, point to the difference between Gatsby and Daisy and their attitudes towards life. Throughout the novel, Gatsby is associated with light, whether it be moonlight, starlight, or artificial lighting. Nick's first sight of Gatsby is one where he sees him 'standing with his hands in his pockets regarding the silver pepper of stars' (p.21). Then, there is Nick's observation of the moon, having 'risen higher' (p.42) as he watches one of his parties in progress. Later, just after Myrtle's death, when Gatsby insists on watching over Daisy's house, Nick sees him 'standing there in the moonlight—watching over nothing' (p.126). Finally, at the close of the novel, Nick's recollection of Gatsby's dream comes in the moonlight:

Most of the big shore places were closed now and there were hardly any lights except the shadowy, moving glow of the ferryboat across the Sound. And as the moon rose higher the inessential houses began to melt away until gradually I became aware of the old island here that flowered once for Dutch sailors' eyes. . . .

And as I sat there brooding on the old, unknown world, I thought of Gatsby's wonder. . . . (pp.155-6)

Artificial lights also provide a setting for Gatsby. His house is usually a blaze of light at night and one night Nick comes home to find Gatsby's house all lit up like the World's Fair.

The two kinds of lights with which Gatsby is associated show up, as it were, the seemingly contradictory character of Gatsby's life at West Egg. The moon image asserts the fantastic and unreal quality of Gatsby's dream. This dream began significantly when he saw Daisy sitting in the porch 'bright with the bought luxury of star-shine' (p.129) just after their sexual experience together. But the artificial lights at his house represent the material means by which he hopes to attract Daisy to his house. The irony lies in the way in which something so idealistic as Gatsby's dream can be achieved by the use of such material devices. Already, Fitzgerald is implying the corruption of Gatsby's ideal, and all because the ideal is Daisy and she is materialistic and worldly. Significantly, therefore, Gatsby's dream shifts from moonlight to the green light at the other end of the dock. He has come to identify this light with Daisy for, compared to the great distance that separates them, the light seems close to her, 'as close as a star to the moon' (p.81). The irony is that Daisy is no moon just as the green light is no star.

If Gatsby is associated with light, Daisy is identified with darkness, or at least with twilight which is near darkness. At her first meeting with Nick at the beginning of the novel, Daisy is seen putting out the candles which have been lit at the dinner table:

'Why candles?' objected Daisy, frowning. She snapped them out with her fingers. (p.14)

Later, according to report, she is seen to turn out the lights as Gatsby watches her house after Myrtle's death. The accident itself occurs at twilight. And when Nick tries to piece together Daisy's life after Gatsby's departure five years ago he writes 'Through this twilight universe Daisy began to move again with the season. . . .' (p.130). The reference to twilight places Daisy in the world of shadows, that is the valley of ashes. They also intensify the absence of that imaginative fire that lights up Gatsby's whole personality. But Gatsby's idealism is snuffed out by Daisy. References to her putting out the lights must, therefore, contain a sinister hint of her ultimate destruction of Gatsby and his dream. Thus it is ironical that in Chapter VII Gatsby has wanted to do without the parties and the lights because he has been reunited with Daisy and does not need to attract her to his house. The failure of the lights to go on, however, seems to anticipate the death of his dream and ideal at Daisy's hands.

The contrast between a materialistic existence and an imaginative life is shown very clearly through two opposing images—'the valley of ashes' (p.23) and the 'fresh, green breast of the new world' (p.155). Seen as a valley of ashes where 'ash-grey men . . . move dimly' (p.23), the materialistic world is represented by barrenness, dryness and unreality. The 'fresh, green breast of the new world', however, taken as an image of the ideal world, associates the mind with a state which is lively, fertile and creative, following the words 'fresh', 'green', and 'breast'.

Gatsby's idealism itself is given a religious, almost divine significance by the way in which he is presented as a god-like figure. Like Christ, he is said to be 'a son of God' who must be 'about His Father's business' (p.86). Notice the way in which Gatsby's first appearance shows him in a gesture of worship: '. . . he stretched out his arms towards the dark water in a curious way. . . .' (p.22) But then this divine image is under-cut by the social and material interests that accompany Gatsby's idealism. His flashy possessions and his unconscious desire for Daisy's social status provide a sharp anticlimax.

Other images that contribute to the effect of the novel are the colour images, which again help to show up the difference between Daisy and Gatsby. Throughout the novel, Daisy is identified with white and silver. When Nick sees Daisy for the first time, she is sitting with Jordan, dressed in white. When Jordan saw Daisy with Gatsby five years ago, she was standing with him beside her white roadster. When Nick arrives with Gatsby at Daisy's house for lunch, she and Jordan are sitting like 'silver idols' (p.100). When Gatsby talks of Daisy five years ago, he describes her as 'gleaming like silver' (p.129).

White and silver are colours that set off the attractiveness and dazzling appeal of Daisy, for these are stark but brilliant colours. The two colours point to the dual aspects of Daisy's character. She is 'white' in her emptiness, her ignorance, because her life is bare of responsibility, involvement or feeling. Silver emphasises her wealth and sophistication, for the colour is associated with glitter and formal polish. White, there-fore, reveals Daisy's mental and moral backwardness, while silver con-veys her physical attractiveness and adult appeal.

Gatsby, of course, is associated with green. Several times he is described as looking at the green light at the end of Daisy's dock. Green being a colour denoting fertility, it is appropriate that it should repre-sent Gatsby's readiness for romance.

Finally, there is the image of Dr Eckleburg's eyes, which conveys a comment on faulty vision. Ironically, and yet not surprisingly, the men in the valley of ashes regard these eyes as the all-seeing eyes of God. Wilson, for one, tells his friend Michaelis that 'God sees everything'. . . . (p.138) Essentially, of course, Wilson is talking of the perception of factual truths rather than of spiritual or even religious truths. In the materialistic world, spectacles may indeed represent the power to see. At the same time, the homage paid to the eyes of Dr Eckleburg may be taken as an indication, in the materialistic world, of man's interest in scientific inventions like spectacles or even in advertisements themselves.

Style

It must not be assumed that a writer's style can be seen in isolation, covering only technical devices such as the choice and use of language, grammatical constructions and so on. For style is very much a part of the total organisation of a piece of writing, it includes the structure, the character presentation, plot and narrative arrangement. Therefore, when we consider Fitzgerald's style in *The Great Gatsby*, we must bear in mind that previous comments on chapter organisation, narrative direction, the use of the actor-narrator, imagery and so on are all relevant to our discussion.

The key to Fitzgerald's style in *The Great Gatsby* is irony. His irony works by way of structure, that is narrative arrangement, and language. From the structural aspect there is

(*a*) juxtaposition that includes the contrast of characters, the balancing of opposing events, the setting off of images against one another and the ironic combination of comic and tragic elements.

(*b*) there is the ironic use of language in the form of cleverly inserted images and phrases to point to some representative quality of a character. Also, there is the construction of descriptive passages that rests on sentence patterns, the choice and arrangement of vocabulary and so on.

In each case, the tone and effect of Fitzgerald's irony varies according to occasion and intention. It ranges from light mockery to bitter criticism or grave comment.

Juxtaposition

Juxtaposition brings about the contrast between the worldly and the idealistic attitudes of the two main groups of characters. The alternating movement of the narrative in the first four chapters keeps these two kinds of extreme behaviour always balanced against one another.

Juxtaposition also plays its part in contrasting the fantastic with the real. This is done in order to mock one or both aspects of life. For example, when Gatsby's sensitivity is described in terms of a seismograph (p.6), the machine image makes fun of his absolute readiness to believe and hope. The seismograph is known for its ability to record the most minute movements of the earth, and Gatsby's idealism is just as ready to grasp at anything that fits into his hopeful outlook. On the other hand, the use of the seismograph image to describe and measure Gatsby's tremendous faith and idealism points mockingly to the materialistic influence of a society that cannot describe a man's imaginative readiness any other way.

This use of a physical/material image to describe idealism is paralleled by the use of fantastic images to describe a physical reality. This is seen when Nick describes the city of New York 'rising up across the river in white heaps and sugar lumps all built with a wish out of non-olfactory money' (p.60). The 'sugar lump' image effectively criticises the shaky appearance of distant sky-scrapers. But the phrase also recalls the sugar lumps out of which houses are built in fairy tales, to lure children into the evil hands of the witch. The image then contains a sinister hint of the hidden dangers of city life, suggesting significantly Nick's subsequent disillusionment with life in the East. The same ironical comment is contained in the similar description of Myrtle's apartment house as 'one slice in a long white cake of apartment-houses' (p.27).

Elsewhere, there is the juxtaposition of the fantastic with the real in a single image, as, for example, when Nick describes Gatsby's need to believe that 'the rock of the world was founded securely on a fairy's wing' (p.86). The use of 'rock' and 'fairy's wing' stresses that Gatsby is trying to make his ideal into reality. But the two images, seen against one another, are totally alien from one another. Gatsby's attempt, therefore, must seem vain and impossible.

Sometimes the juxtaposition of two images helps to anticipate the final outcome of later events. When Nick, at the beginning of Chapter I, refers to the 'foul dust [that] floated in the wake of [Gatsby's] dreams' (p.6), the dust image together with 'foul' contrasts at once with Gatsby's dreams, suggesting, therefore, the atmosphere of death and ashes that threaten Gatsby's idealism. The fact that the word 'wake' apart from meaning 'rear' (thus 'behind') also means 'funeral rite' increases the suggestion of death even more.

Although *The Great Gatsby* is essentially a tragic novel, Fitzgerald's narrative is by no means lacking in comedy and humour. While the comic scenes are often meant to enhance the tragic tone of the novel by means of contrast, they provide a welcome relief of tension at crucial points. They also comment on the action that is taking place.

In some cases the comic scenes paradoxically hold a hint of tragedy. This tragic element usually stems from the fact that the scene, however comically described, actually looks forward to later disastrous developments. A typical example is the comic scene in Chapter II, where Myrtle is seen holding a party in her apartment in New York. The light-heartedness of the incident contrasts with Nick's growing unease at this spectacle of Tom's infidelity. Meanwhile, Myrtle's efforts to play the role of a society hostess, with her careless gossip and her artificial behaviour, hide a desperate desire to escape from her own class. And the grotesque incident when she fights with Tom over her use of Daisy's name contains a hidden warning, because it anticipates her death at the hands of Tom and Daisy.

An even more striking incident is that when Gatsby meets Daisy for the first time after five years. The scene is full of comedy as Nick describes the absurd behaviour of Gatsby and himself as both are overcome by nervousness and embarrassment. On Gatsby's part, the ridiculous behaviour continues when his anxiety gives way to ecstasy and excitement. The comedy has the immediate effect of easing the tense atmosphere but at the same time it indirectly shows up the significance that the scene holds for Gatsby. It is because the event means so much to him that he behaves so absurdly. Nick's behaviour, however, is caused by his concern and his feeling of sympathy for Gatsby. If this scene is compared to some earlier ones where Gatsby appears aloof and correct, it is clear that his very absurdity here indicates his actual state of intense yearning and need.

On the other hand, the comedy in this scene contrasts ironically with the tragedy that ultimately occurs. And what is even more ironical is that it is this very comic scene of Gatsby's reunion with Daisy that brings about the final destruction of Gatsby at the end. Viewed in this way, the comic scene is horribly ironical. And there are several such scenes for example, the funny car accident in which Owl-eyes is mistaken for the driver, and the event where Gatsby is snubbed by Tom and the Sloanes.

The other aspect of Fitzgerald's irony involves the use of language. First of all there is the insertion of single images or phrases to capture the most striking quality that identifies a character. One example of this is the description of Tom's physical attributes and his materialistic outlook in terms of a single image. This is seen where Nick describes Tom in a slang phrase 'I think he'd tanked up a good deal at luncheon . . .' (p.24). 'Tanked' aptly conveys Tom's drinking habits which are indicative of his reckless, pleasurable way of living. The image, however, implying fuel and power as it does, describes Tom as if he were a motor-car so that at once there is the suggestion of Tom's physical, muscular power on the one hand, and of his lavish, up-to-date material possessions on the other. With the use of one single image, therefore, Tom's whole way of life and personality are conveyed.

In another case, when Myrtle fights with Tom over her use of Daisy's name, she is described by Nick as 'bleeding fluently' (p.35). The word 'fluently' that comes with 'bleeding' seems unsuitable, but it is in fact a mocking comment, that the fight causes more fuss and noise from Myrtle than the actual injuries she receives from Tom.

Apart from all this, irony helps Fitzgerald to write with a good amount of humour. The laughter and amusement that is brought about is usually achieved by the device of comic exaggeration. Notice the way in which Gatsby's garden, lighted up for a party, is compared to a Christmas tree (p.36). Elsewhere, his house is said to resemble the

World's Fair (p.71), and Nick, seeing it from afar, is driven into a panic, thinking that his own house is on fire. Fitzgerald's use of names to comment on the characters can also be funny. In the social commentary in Chapter IV, for example, the New Yorkers are given such names as Newton Orchid, Ernest Lilly, Ferret, S.W. Belcher, the Smirkes, Miss Hag, Claudia Hip and so on. This kind of comedy gives Fitzgerald's writing an added sparkle and life which is highly appealing.

Irony plays a prominent part in controlling the way in which Fitzgerald constructs, organises, and describes his scenes and characters. But there is also his skill in vivid presentation which comes by way of his choice of language and grammatical construction. This kind of effective portrayal is what lifts Nick's narrative from a mere recording of events. Fitzgerald very often writes in a sharp, racy style that evokes the atmosphere of a scene quite effortlessly. This is seen especially in the description of Gatsby's parties:

> The lights grow brighter as the earth lurches away from the sun, and now the orchestra is playing yellow cocktail music, and the opera of voices pitches a key higher. Laughter is easier minute by minute, spilled with prodigality, tipped out at a cheerful word. The groups change more swiftly, swell with new arrivals, dissolve and form in the same breath; already there are wanderers, confident girls who weave here and there among the stouter and more stable, become for a sharp, joyous moment the centre of a group, and then, excited with triumph, glide on through the sea-change of faces and voices and colour under the constantly changing light.
>
> Suddenly one of these gypsies, in trembling opal, seizes a cocktail out of the air, dumps it down for courage and, moving her hands like Frisco, dances out alone on the canvas platform. A momentary hush; the orchestra leader varies his rhythm obligingly for her, and there is a burst of chatter as the erroneous news goes around that she is Gilda Gray's understudy from the Follies. The party has begun. (p.37)

This description has a poetic quality for it catches at once the brilliance and pulsing beat of movement and voices. Fitzgerald projects the shifting disorder of the scene very vividly.

The scene is first looked at from a distance and the view is wide, covering a broad picture of general gaiety. In the first paragraph, the broad description creates an impression of a vague faceless crowd, identified only by the sounds of laughter and by movements. The use of such words of movement like 'lurches', 'swell', 'dissolve', 'form' and 'glide' mingle with the choice of words describing sound, but which actually are associated with movement also—words like 'spilled' and 'tipped'. Together they build up the atmosphere of restlessness and disorder. Most of these words are also associated with drunkenness, and this increases the sense of chaos and reckless enjoyment even more.

The second paragraph continues with a closer view of the party, and picks out the drunken display of one of the girls. Here the style is more dramatic, to fit the stage-like scene which is being played out. The description is now brisk and sharp. The short sentences and the effective pauses are used successfully to achieve the sense of attentiveness and expectation among the guests.

Fitzgerald also combines this kind of poetic representation with a more relaxed kind of description. The latter is especially obvious in the dialogue scenes, where the tone is usually light and careless. The idle gossip and chatter of Daisy and her friends, for example, are typical, even though these scenes do usually hold some ironic significance. Elsewhere, in Gatsby's conversations, the style is more deliberate and the tone is heavy with underlying anxieties and implications.

Fitzgerald, then, uses a variety of styles in *The Great Gatsby*. The overall impression, however, is a lively, informal style that flows easily and with natural ease.

Characters in the novel

Nick Carraway

Apart from the fact that there are two main groups of characters, that is, Gatsby and the Buchanans, there is also the person of the narrator who is not totally detached from the action. It is true that Nick Carraway begins by merely recording events and keeping a distance between himself and characters such as the Buchanans and Gatsby. But he is soon caught up with the people and the events around him. His getting tipsy at Myrtle's party is perhaps the first indication that he cannot remain unaffected by what goes on. And he soon becomes more intimate with Jordan, a sure sign of his growing involvement. In Chapter V, with his arrangement of the meeting between Daisy and Gatsby and his sensitivity to Gatsby's feelings, Nick becomes totally committed. And in the remaining chapters, his sympathy for Gatsby grows until he not only feels responsible for him at his burial; he understands what Gatsby stands for. All this, however, does not mean that Nick can be totally identified with Gatsby against the Buchanans. For Nick preserves a rational frame of mind that makes him also realise what is wrong with Gatsby. And unlike Gatsby, whose personality remains unchanging and static, Nick develops and matures. While Gatsby and the Buchanans guard their interests single-mindedly, Nick learns to see matters from others' points of view. The last meeting with Jordan when she accuses him of having been careless and cruel with her, makes him realise how things must look from a point of view other than his own. And his last meeting with Tom convinces Nick that things are not necessarily as he sees them. Tom has his own way of looking at his actions.

Nick is not to be placed with Gatsby or with the Buchanans, for he stands alone and above them. Nick, indeed, is the real protagonist in the novel, not Gatsby. For Gatsby and the Buchanans represent two kinds of extreme behaviour, two distorted ways of life. Gatsby may dominate over the Buchanans because his values are more appealing, but his view of life still remains one-sided and unreal. Nick, however, achieves moral insight and wisdom, which make him a more complete person. Indirectly then, the novel, through the events concerning Gatsby and the Buchanans, traces Nick's development, from detachment to participation, from passive unconcern to understanding, from a narrow, subjective outlook to a broad indulgence.

Jay Gatsby

The character of Jay Gatsby is mystifying because it contains so many contradictory qualities. On the one hand he is heroic, larger than ordinary men, but on the other he is trivial and common. Gatsby is sensitive and idealistic, almost divine in his dedication to his love and faith. But he is also sinister, because of his criminal activities. He is aloof and self-sufficient at his parties, but he is also absurd (as with Mrs Sloane), vulgar and flashy (as in the way he shows off his possessions). His inconsistent character, together with his uncertain background, is hard to define. All this, however, helps to create the impression of a remote figure, and this is in keeping with the unreal, fantastic atmosphere that surrounds him and his dream.

Seen in its fantastic immensity, Gatsby's dream, that is his life and his love for Daisy, becomes a lofty, magnificent plan that cannot be denied. Yet ironically Daisy herself is far from ideal. Her voice is 'full of money' (p.104) and she plays at love like a child.

Significantly, however, in spite of all the inconsistencies and contradictions, Gatsby manages to hold the reader's sympathy throughout. The whole-hearted dedication of Gatsby and his sincere belief in what he does makes him heroic, and this submerges the unpleasant details so that they do not seem important in the final outcome.

Daisy Fay

Daisy's character is built around two conflicting factors. There is first her physical appeal which goes to create an image of beauty, wealth and innocence. For Gatsby, who originally belongs to a poorer back-

ground and a lower social class, the rich, youthful radiance that surrounds Daisy contains a promise of perfect love and happiness:

> . . . Gatsby was overwhelmingly aware of the youth and mystery that
> wealth imprisons and preserves, of the freshness of many clothes,
> and of Daisy, gleaming like silver, safe and proud above the hot
> struggles of the poor. (p.129)

For Gatsby then, Daisy becomes the dream of a lifetime—an image of
excellence and perfection which is utterly remote to a penniless young
man. Nick describes Gatsby's view of Daisy thus: 'High in a white
palace the king's daughter, the golden girl . . .' (p.104). The name 'Daisy'
matches the 'flower-like' (p.21), sweet-scented beauty and youthfulness
that the girl represents. Her other name 'Fay', being a pun on 'fey',
holds a suggestion of being fairy-like, thus enhancing Daisy's magical
appeal.

Whatever her physical image, however, Daisy's character contains a
darker, less attractive side. She is not only flighty and trivial, but also
selfish, ruthlessly using others for her own ends. Indeed she is morally
destructive because she is irresponsible and acts without conscience.
Her physical attractiveness, then, with its empty promise, is merely a
trick, and Gatsby is caught, trapped in her spell. Daisy indeed is more
of a witch than a fairy.* Her magic has an evil influence. It destroys
and kills.

Tom Buchanan

Tom Buchanan is cast as Gatsby's opposite in the novel. Right from
the beginning, in Chapter I, Tom's physical power and athletic activities
are made obvious. These, together with his wealth and material possessions, place him against Gatsby's sentimental outlook. Whereas Gatsby
yearns for love and beauty, Tom, as Nick puts it, seeks 'wistfully, for the
dramatic turbulence of some irrecoverable football game' (p.9). If
Gatsby is given to fantasy, Tom is absorbed in very earthly pursuits.

Like Daisy and even like Gatsby, there is something childish about
Tom and his excessive concern with his own interests. When he finds
that things are not moving to his favour, he is determined to arrange
things to suit himself, no matter whom he hurts in the process. When
he finds out about Gatsby's interest in his wife, for example, Tom is
quick to force Gatsby to a showdown. It is not certain that Tom wants
Daisy because he loves her. Whether he or Daisy is capable of loving
anyone but themselves is questionable. His desire to keep his wife may
just reflect the pride of a man who refuses to have his wife taken away

*This point is made in Leslie Fiedler, *Love and Death in the American Novel*, Stein and Day,
New York, 1973, pp.312–3.

from him by another man. And added to this pride is Tom's social consciousness. To surrender Daisy to a man who is his social inferior is too humiliating to bear. Gatsby, therefore, finds himself up against Tom's ruthlessness and social arrogance.

Tom, however, does not only smash up Gatsby's dream. After the accident, Gatsby's sentimental outlook prevents him from safeguarding himself against blame. Tom is quick to take advantage of this. He makes Gatsby bear the responsibility for Myrtle's death so as to save Daisy. There is a close bond between him and Daisy after all; they are not only husband and wife but members of the same social group. And so Tom does not only destroy Gatsby's idealism, he also takes Gatsby's life. That Tom is able to defeat Gatsby so easily, and goes unpunished, points to the fact that, in a materialistic society, people like Tom, rich, ruthless and cunning, will always triumph. Idealism and sentimentality, especially when carried to the extreme, are sure to be taken advantage of by others.

Jordan Baker

Jordan's role in the novel is a complex one. First, she is the second narrator who describes Gatsby's early relationship with Daisy. In this account, she obviously mocks Daisy's fickle behaviour and her fluctuating relationship with her husband afterwards. In this way, Jordan is not just a narrator but a commentator as well, and her account, coming through Nick, helps to place the early Gatsby-Daisy relationship further away from the reader, thus increasing the sense of its unreality.

Elsewhere, Jordan is a reflection of Daisy. Her cheating at golf, her careless driving, and her quick departure from Daisy's house after the accident prepare the reader for Daisy's betrayal and desertion of Gatsby. Jordan, with her quick cynical observation of Daisy's inability to remain faithful to Gatsby after his departure five years ago and her comments on Tom's infidelity, is set against Gatsby's idealistic belief in perfect love and happiness with Daisy. In other words, Jordan is juxtaposed against Gatsby.

The Nick-Jordan relationship provides a sub-plot that parallels the Gatsby-Daisy relationship. But while Gatsby's love for Daisy is related to an ideal, Nick's relationship with Jordan shows his attraction to Jordan's world, that is the world of careless enjoyment and idle pursuits. And it is ironical that Jordan should accuse Nick of having treated her carelessly, for she herself belongs to the thoughtless, uncaring crowd which takes advantage of other people's vulnerability.

Part 4

Hints for study

Points for close study

(1) See how Nick's comment at the end of Chapter IX (p.156) relates to the theme of the novel.

(2) Consider the way in which the novel is related to the American Dream.

(3) Study the way in which Chapter V, the meeting between Gatsby and Daisy, brings the earlier part of the action (contained in Chapters I to IV) to a climax. See how Chapter VII brings the second part of the action, from Chapter V on, to its climax. Which do you think is the real turning point in the novel: Chapter V or Chapter VII?

(4) Examine the juxtaposition of Gatsby and the Buchanans in Chapters I to IV.

(5) Examine closely the setting in the Buchanans' house in Chapter I. See also the effectiveness of the setting in Myrtle's apartment in Chapter II. Note the references to Gatsby's extravagant and flashy possessions.

(6) Consider the way in which the history of Gatsby's life is given in fragments throughout the novel.

Significant quotations

Certain quotations reveal very clearly the character of a person or his attitude at a particular point in the plot. Others indicate the crucial moments or climaxes in the action. Classifying these quotations in these ways and memorising parts of them will help to save time and bother when it comes to revision and answering questions in examinations.

QUOTATIONS REVEALING CHARACTER

Nick

The following quotations show Nick's change in attitude:

And so with the sunshine and the great bursts of leaves growing on the trees, . . . I had that familiar conviction that life was beginning over again with the summer. (p.7)

Thirty—the promise of a decade of loneliness, a thinning list of single men to know, a thinning brief-case of enthusiasm, thinning hair. (p.117)

Gatsby

The truth was that Jay Gatsby of West Egg, Long Island, sprang from his Platonic conception of himself. He was a son of God . . . and he must be about His Father's business, the service of a vast, vulgar and meretricious beauty. (p.86)

. . . Gatsby was overwhelmingly aware of the youth and mystery that wealth imprisons and preserves, of the freshness of many clothes, and of Daisy, gleaming like silver, safe and proud above the hot struggles of the poor. (p.129)

Gatsby believed in the green light, the orgiastic future that year by year recedes before us. (p.156)

Daisy

. . . there was an excitement in her voice . . ., a promise that she had done gay, exciting things just a while since and that there were gay, exciting things hovering in the next hour. (p.12)

'What'll we do with ourselves this afternoon?' cried Daisy, 'and the day after that, and the next thirty years?' (p.102)

High in a white palace the king's daughter, the golden girl . . . (p.104)

They were careless people, Tom and Daisy—they smashed up things and creatures and then retreated back into their money or their vast carelessness . . . and let other people clean up the mess they had made . . . (p.154)

Tom

It was a body capable of enormous leverage—a cruel body. (p.10)

His speaking voice . . . added to the impression of fractiousness he conveyed. There was a touch of paternal contempt in it, even towards people he liked . . . (p.10)

I couldn't forgive him or like him, but I saw that what he had done was, to him, entirely justified. It was all very careless and confused. (p.154)

Jordan

She was incurably dishonest . . . I suppose she had begun dealing in subterfuges when she was very young in order to keep that cool, insolent smile turned to the world and yet satisfy the demands of her hard, jaunty body. (p.52)

. . . this clean, hard, limited person, who dealt in universal scepticism . . . (p.70)

TURNING POINTS IN THE NOVEL

Nick's understanding of Gatsby

'Gatsby bought that house so that Daisy would be just across the bay.'
Then it had not been merely the stars to which he had aspired on that June night. He came alive to me, delivered suddenly from the womb of his purposeless splendour. (p.69)

Gatsby's longing for Daisy

As I went over to say goodbye I saw that the expression of bewilderment had come back into Gatsby's face, as though a faint doubt had occurred to him as to the quality of his present happiness. Almost five years! There must have been moments even that afternoon when Daisy tumbled short of his dreams—not through her own fault, but because of the colossal vitality of his illusion. (p.83)

'Oh, you want too much!' she cried to Gatsby. 'I love you now—isn't that enough? I can't help what's past.' She began to sob helplessly. 'I did love him once—but I loved you too.' (p.114)

Moral comment

And as I sat there brooding on the old, unknown world, I thought of Gatsby's wonder when he first picked out the green light at the end of Daisy's dock. He had come a long way to this blue lawn, and his dream must have seemed so close that he could hardly fail to grasp it. He did not know that it was already behind him, somewhere back in that vast obscurity beyond the city, where the dark fields of the republic rolled on under the night.

Gatsby believed in the green light, the orgiastic future that year by year recedes before us. It eluded us then, but that's no matter—tomorrow we will run faster, stretch out our arms farther . . . And one fine morning—

So we beat on, boats against the current, borne back ceaselessly into the past. (p.156)

Answering questions

The following notes relate to questions which require discussion and contextual knowledge.

The first requirement in answering any question in an examination is a thorough knowledge of the text. After this, the ability to select and apply material effectively in answers is needed. This skill, however, can be acquired through training. There are two stages of preparation that one must be aware of in order to answer a question well.

First of all, you have to understand the question. This is not as simple as it sounds. In many cases, it may mean that the key words or phrases have to be defined on different levels, in order to indicate the angles or points of view from which the question will be discussed. Definition of an ambiguous word or a sweeping statement also helps to determine the exact area that will be covered. But we cannot just define what is given in a question. We sometimes have to be clear about what is implied as well. Take the following question for example:

Who is the real hero in *The Great Gatsby*: Gatsby or Nick Carraway? Give specific and cogent reasons for your choice.

In this case, the definition of the word 'hero' is not enough. It is necessary to differentiate between the 'real' hero and the 'false' hero, as it is so implied. The choice of Gatsby or Nick as the 'real' hero will depend on the definition of these terms.

When it comes to the organisation of materials from the text, it is necessary first of all to determine the nature of the question that is asked. If the question relates to the main theme of the novel, then this theme must be seen in relation to all the main characters. That is, one has to show how the different characters relate one way or another to the main idea in the novel. This would be relevant in a question like the following:

How is the theme of love related to the theme of money in *The Great Gatsby*?

The concern with love and money makes up the main idea in the novel. How love and money are related to each other in the case of each of the characters will constitute the substance of the answer. However, characters, for whom love is not related with money, must not be omitted. Nick's sympathy for Gatsby, if it is not love in the sexual sense, is still relevant in that it is love seen in a wider aspect, meaning fellow-feeling. And if Nick's feeling for Gatsby is unrelated to money, this helps to mark a clear contrast between him and all the other characters for whom money must always affect ideas of love.

If the theme picked on is not the main one but a minor one instead, then it is still necessary to see how the various characters are involved in this subsidiary theme. And on top of this, you have to go on to show how this minor idea running through the novel is connected to and helps the main theme. An example of a minor theme is that relating to social awareness and class discrimination in *The Great Gatsby*. A question concerning this may come as follows:

To what extent is *The Great Gatsby* a story about class and social discrimination?

If the given question involves a character's position or role in the novel, the way to go about it is to see the character in terms of what happens. That is, one has to consider what the character does and how this relates him to the main stream of events or theme. Also, it is relevant to examine how other characters relate to him, how he sees them, and how they regard him. It is also advisable to compare his initial position or attitude with his final standpoint. Is this change, if there is a change, for the better or for the worse? A suitable question may come simply like the following:

What kind of a girl is Daisy?

If a question relates to some aspect of style or structure, it is always helpful to re-state the theme first of all. After this, you have to go on to show how the organisation or language used connect with the main theme. It is useless to talk about the arrangement of events or the use of imagery in isolation from the theme because this will not show up their significance in the work as a whole. For all the various parts of the novel should cohere, to achieve a successful and effective piece of writing. If any aspect of the writing or organisation seems separate from the other parts, then the work is weak and badly put together.

As regards context questions, after the identification of the speaker/s or the character/s involved, there is a need to place the event correctly within the text. It is immaterial whether or not the time of occurrence of the event is specifically asked for. The knowledge of what has preceded the event and what comes after will help to bring about an understanding of the significance of the episode referred to, in relation to the whole plot. For a context question does require that the connection between the given event and the total action be clearly indicated and explained. And if possible, the given incident should be related not only to the theme, but also to the structure of the novel, that is, the event should be seen in terms of the total design and arrangement of episodes. You have to show how the scene that is given fits in.

Take, for example, Nick's description of Gatsby's early ambitions and achievements in Chapter VI. It is not enough just to say that the function of the passage is to develop such ideas as Gatsby's idealism and heroic determination. The placing of Nick's account, in relation to other events in the novel, must be considered, in order to measure the full impact of the description given here. Coming at the beginning of Chapter VI, the details of Gatsby's optimism occur immediately after his first meeting with Daisy after five years. At the point when his dream of Daisy seems about to be realised, therefore, Nick describes how Gatsby's life and identity are built on faith and hope. His desire for Daisy, then, must be seen to be a part of a larger dream. From Nick's account, it is clear that, so far, Gatsby's idealism has not met with any set-backs. Now, the outcome of his relationship with Daisy will either increase his faith or else destroy his life and identity altogether. Therefore, when the moment of decision comes in Chapter VII, when Daisy has to choose between Tom and Gatsby, the urgency of the situation is all the more intense. If Daisy fails him, Gatsby's confidence in himself and his life will be shattered. Nick's account of Gatsby and his life, occurring where it does, makes this abundantly clear.

Specimen questions and model answers

Discussive questions

(1) Who is the real hero of *The Great Gatsby* : Gatsby or Nick Carraway? Give specific and cogent reasons for your choice.
(2) Discuss in detail Gatsby's vision of reality and the place that Daisy has in it. Is this vision essentially tragic or what?
(3) How is the theme of love related with the theme of money in *The Great Gatsby*?
(4) 'Nick Carraway was taken in; Gatsby was a vulgar, sentimental, immoral fraud.' Discuss.
(5) 'Gatsby is a remarkable conception, convincing because we see him through the eyes of Carraway.' Discuss this statement.
(6) Is there a hero in *The Great Gatsby*?
(7) Analyse Nick Carraway's moral development in *The Great Gatsby*.
(8) Discuss the methods in which the history of Gatsby's life is related to the reader.
(9) Give a close account of the Gatsby-Carraway relationship. Show how it contributes to our understanding of the novel.
(10) 'Fitzgerald's single great theme is the theme of sentimental education.' Discuss with reference to *The Great Gatsby*.

Questions on content

(1) Describe Nick's first visit to Daisy's house. What are his impressions of Tom and Daisy?
(2) From the occasional bits of information given throughout the novel, give a full account of Gatsby's life, from the time he was seventeen to the time of his meeting with Daisy again.
(3) Describe Gatsby's meeting with Daisy in Nick's house and compare their different reactions.

(4) Relate the events that lead to Gatsby's death.

(5) Give an outline of the Nick-Jordan relationship and compare it with the Daisy-Gatsby affair.

Context questions

For each of the extracts given below, name the speaker/s and show how each quotation relates significantly to the plot.

(1) 'My dear,' she cried, 'I'm going to give you this dress as soon as I'm through with it. I've got to get another one tomorrow. I'm going to make a list of all the things I've got to get. A massage and a wave, and a collar for the dog, and one of those cute little ash-trays where you touch a spring, and a wreath with a black silk bow for mother's grave that'll last all summer. I got to write down a list so I won't forget all the things I got to do.' (p.34)

(2) The modesty of the demand shook me. He had waited five years and bought a mansion where he dispensed starlight to casual moths —so that he could 'come over' some afternoon to a stranger's garden. (p.69)

(3) 'Can't repeat the past?' he cried incredulously. 'Why of course you can!' (p.96)

(4) 'I spoke to her,' he muttered, after a long silence. 'I told her she might fool me but she couldn't fool God. I took her to the window'— with an effort he got up and walked to the rear window and leaned with his face pressed against it—'and I said "God knows what you've been doing, everything you've been doing. You may fool me but you can't fool God."' (p.138)

(5) 'I told him the truth,' he said. 'He came to the door while we were getting ready to leave, and when I sent word that we weren't in he tried to force his way upstairs. He was crazy enough to kill me if I hadn't told him who owned the car. His hand was on a revolver in his pocket every minute he was in the house—' He broke off defiantly. 'What if I did tell him? That fellow had it coming to him. He threw dust into your eyes just like he did in Daisy's, but he was a tough one. He ran over Myrtle like you'd run over a dog and never even stopped his car.' (p.154)

Model answers to discussive questions

Is there a hero in *The Great Gatsby*?

The word 'hero' usually means a character who dominates the action, in that everything that happens centres around him; it is he, in fact, who gives rise to the events that take place. It is possible that sometimes in a novel, there is no hero, in the sense that there is no single character around whom the plot revolves. This usually happens in a social satire or a novel of manners, where the interest is in a whole society or a community and its behaviour. George Eliot's *Middlemarch* and Thackeray's *Vanity Fair* are two examples of such novels that have no heroes.

In *The Great Gatsby*, however, the presence of a prominent character, one who is central to the events that occur, cannot be denied. Gatsby is the character who causes the action in the novel. It is his dream of Daisy, his desire to re-establish their former relationship, that gives rise to Nick's involvement, Tom's hostility and the deaths of Myrtle and Gatsby himself. And it is Gatsby, with his idealism and unquestioning faith, who predominates in the reader's imagination and wins his sympathy and awe. It would seem then that not only does the novel have a hero but that the hero is Gatsby himself.

However, we must remember that Gatsby represents only one side of the moral theme. He must always be seen against the Buchanans. The action does not merely involve the events that happen—the action concerns the balancing of two ways of life, two sets of values as represented by Gatsby and the Buchanans. And it is Nick Carraway, as he moves between these two groups of characters, who achieves a greater significance. Through his reactions and comments, he shows up the attractiveness and shortcomings of each way of life. In so doing he develops the kind of maturity towards which the whole moral theme of the novel is moving. And although Gatsby captures the reader's imagination, it is Nick with whom he identifies himself. It is through Nick too that the reader is able to see Gatsby's magnificence as well as his vulgarity. The novel's hero, therefore, is not Gatsby but Nick Carraway.

Justify, refute or qualify Fitzgerald's calling his protagonist 'The Great Gatsby'.

Gatsby's 'greatness' refers to that heroic quality about him that lifts him above the level of ordinary men. It is not just his material success, his wonderful capacity to live up to his desire for success, that distinguishes him. It is true that he has come a long way, materially speaking, from the shores of Lake Superior to New York, from being a clam-digger to being a wealthy businessman to whom the police-commissioner sends a Christmas card every year. His determination and persistence, as confirmed by the work schedule that his father shows Nick, is, on its own, admirable. But material success, however hard-earned, is not really awe-inspiring, especially when it is compared to that of so many others in New York who are also wealthy. Gatsby's greatness, his heroism, lies in his immense faith in himself and in life's opportunities. He sees himself as a god-like figure, destined for 'great achievements and great happiness. It is this idealistic attitude that has motivated his material success in the first place. And it is this idealism again that encourages his dream of Daisy and his desire to repeat the past. His sense of purpose is unwavering, and, in a way, he almost manages to sweep Daisy along with his intense faith and sincerity.

Seen against the idle, meaningless existence of the Buchanans and other New Yorkers, Gatsby's idealism becomes definitely heroic in contrast. Even his restlessness is associated with a sense of determination and ambition. With the others, however, there is 'the absence of all desire' (p.14). Whereas Tom and Daisy drift about among their kind of people, Gatsby's movements are all planned for a purpose. Even his wild parties, therefore, are not mere wasteful events.

Gatsby's magnificence, however, is offset by his vulgarity. In spite of his desire for perfect love and happiness, he is still very much aware of his money and material possessions. The desire to show these off betrays a corruption of his idealised concern with love and his own heroic destiny. But the fact that Gatsby's dream has come to centre around Daisy already shows a lowering of his idealised idea of love and happiness. For Daisy is essentially materialistic, concerned with money and physical things. By making her the centre of his dream, Gatsby's heroic stature is reduced. His ideal is not so lofty and noble after all. Indeed, his love for Daisy, his idealisation of her, stems from a consciousness of her wealth and social status. The whole noble significance of Gatsby's ideal therefore, is tarnished by the fact that this ideal is Daisy.

Still, Gatsby's wonder, his 'gift for hope' places him above the Buchanans. His idealism is a creative force when compared with the destructive irresponsibility of Daisy and Tom. And as Nick tells him towards the end,

'They're a rotten crowd . . . You're worth the whole damn bunch put together.'

Answers to context questions

For the extract given below, name the speaker/s and show how the passage relates significantly to the plot.

'She didn't like it,' he insisted. 'She didn't have a good time.'

He was silent, and I guessed at his unutterable depression.

'I feel far away from her,' he said. 'It's hard to make her understand.'

'You mean about the dance?'

'The dance?' He dismissed all the dances he had given with a snap of his fingers. 'Old sport, the dance is unimportant.' (p.95)

Gatsby is here speaking to Nick. They have just said goodbye to Daisy and Tom who have come to one of Gatsby's parties for the first time. It is some time after the reunion between Gatsby and Daisy and this is the first occasion that Gatsby sees Daisy with her husband, Tom. His depression after the party is not so much over the fact that Daisy has not enjoyed herself. What troubles him more is the sight of Daisy going off with her husband. Daisy has not yet given him any sign that their relationship (hers and Gatsby's) will lead to anything. Gatsby is impatient for Daisy to act, to leave her husband and marry him. But all Daisy does is to come to his party with Tom and go off again with him.

Gatsby's words here are very significant. It is ironical that he should complain about Daisy's lack of understanding because later events will show that Daisy is certainly ignorant about Gatsby's idealism. She does not and can not see that Gatsby's feelings for her are part of a total faith in life. From her materialistic world, filled with shallow pursuits, Daisy is a stranger to the kind of sensitivity and devotion that Gatsby represents. Gatsby, therefore, is bound for disappointment at the hands of a girl who does not share his 'gift for hope'. But when Gatsby says that he feels 'far away from her' he is thinking of that moment of impatience only. He has no idea that he will always be far away from Daisy, that she will never understand him.

Part 5

Suggestions for further reading

The text

SCOTT FITZGERALD, F.: *The Great Gatsby*, with commentary and notes by J.F. Wyatt, The Bodley Head Series, London, 1967. The brief notes and analysis of the text provided in this edition are of great help to students since they point out quickly and clearly the main items of interest in the novel.

SCOTT FITZGERALD, F.: *The Great Gatsby*, with foreword and study guide by Albert K. Ridout, Charles Scribner's Sons, New York, 1961. Gives a less full commentary than that of J.F. Wyatt in The Bodley Head Series, 1967

Other works by Scott Fitzgerald

This Side of Paradise Charles Scribner's Sons, New York, 1920.
Flappers and Philosophers Charles Scribner's Sons, New York, 1921.
The Beautiful and Damned Charles Scribner's Sons, New York, 1922.
Tales of the Jazz Age Charles Scribner's Sons, New York, 1922.
All the Sad Young Men Charles Scribner's Sons, New York, 1926.
Tender is the Night Charles Scribner's Sons, New York, 1934.
Taps at Reveille Charles Scribner's Sons, New York, 1935.
The Last Tycoon, edited by Edmund Wilson, Charles Scribner's Sons, New York, 1941.
The Crack-Up, edited by Edmund Wilson, New Directions, New York, 1945.
The Stories of F. Scott Fitzgerald, introduced by Malcolm Cowley, Charles Scribner's Sons, New York, 1951.
Afternoon of an Author: A Selection of Uncollected Stories and Essays, introduction and notes by Arthur Mizener, Princeton University Library, Princeton, New Jersey, 1957.
The Pat Hobby Stories, edited by Arnold Gingrich, Charles Scribner's Son's New York, 1962.
The Letters of F. Scott Fitzgerald, edited and introduced by Andrew Turnbull, Penguin Books, Harmondsworth, 1968.
Paperback editions of *This Side of Paradise, The Great Gatsby, Tender is the Night, The Last Tycoon, The Crack-Up, The Letters of F. Scott Fitzgerald* are published by Penguin Books, Harmondsworth.

General reading

Background
ALLEN, WALTER, *The Urgent West: The American Dream and Modern Man*, E.P. Dutton, New York, 1969.

Biographies
MIZENER, ARTHUR: *The Far Side of Paradise*, Eyre and Spottiswood, London, 1951.
PIPER, H. DAN: *Scott Fitzgerald: A Critical Biography*, The Bodley Head, London, 1966. Includes a critical appraisal of Fitzgerald's works.

Critical studies
CHASE, RICHARD: *The American Novel and its Tradition*, G. Bell and Sons, London, 1958. Contains an interesting study of *The Great Gatsby* as a novel of manners.
HOFFMAN, FREDERICK J. (EDITOR): *The Great Gatsby: A Study*, Charles Scribner's Sons, New York, 1962. A good collection of critical essays on the novel.
LEHAN, RICHARD D.: *F. Scott Fitzgerald and the Craft of Fiction*, Southern Illinois University Press, Carbondale, 1972. This gives an insight into Fitzgerald's character, background and work.
MIZENER, ARTHUR (EDITOR): *Scott Fitzgerald: A Collection of Critical Essays*, Prentice-Hall, Englewood Cliffs, New Jersey, 1963. A useful collection of essays on Fitzgerald and his works.
Modern Fiction Studies, I, No.1 (Spring 1961). This is a special number on F. Scott Fitzgerald.

The author of these notes

TANG SOO PING M.A., was formerly a teacher who taught English to Sixth Form students. At present, she is a lecturer in English at the University of Malaya, and is currently writing a study of Lawrence Durrell's two later novels, *Tunc* and *Nunquam*.